MAKING S#!T HAPPEN

The 5 Pillars of Awesome

By

Carl Pate

Dedications

To my wonderful wife, Andrea for your unwavering support of all of my crazy ideas and for editing out all of my unending waffle!!

And to Phoenix & McKenzie. You are absolutely amazing. You have the world at your feet and your whole life ahead of you. Don't waste a single minute of it.

Disclaimer

ISBN: 978-1-9999691-3-4

First published in 2018

CONTENTS

Sweat the Small Stuff
H
A
B
I
T
S
A
L
I
G
N
M
E
N
T
B
A
L
A
N
C
E
I
N
T
E
G
R
A
T
I
O
N
T
R
A
C
K
I
N
G
The 5 Pillars of Awesome

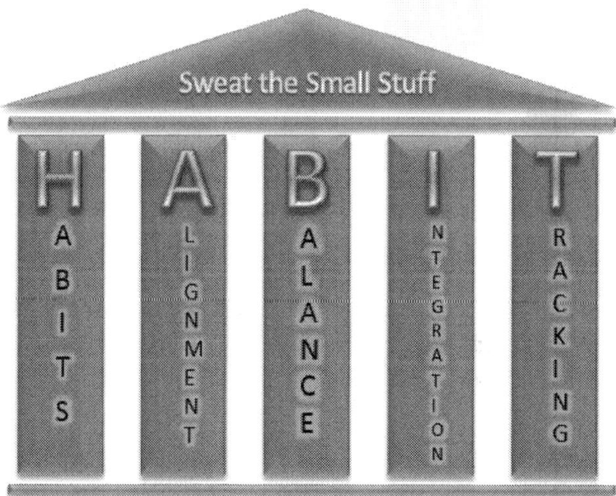

Introduction

Introduction

I hate time wasting and, for me, regret is the most repulsive of all emotions. We have one life and, even at its longest, this is over in the bat of an eye. So why do so many people struggle to motivate themselves into action? Over the last 20 years or more I have become obsessed with time and how we get the very most from it. But don't be mistaken into thinking that this is all about the big stuff. It isn't. Much of what I will talk about in this book is easily accessible to everyone and will give you a powerful sense of self that changes not only the way that you look at life, but also the way that you go about it.

Time is our most valuable resource. Once it's gone, it's gone.

Within the pages that follow I am going to introduce you to my system for taking control of your time, and ultimately your life. I call it The 5 Pillars of Awesome™. These are the Pillars on which you can build a life of meaning and significance as you learn to take advantage of the most precious gift that we have been given – **TIME**.

Here are the Pillars:

- Habit
- Alignment
- Balance
- Integration
- Tracking

The first three Pillars – Habit, Alignment and Balance – are foundational. This is where you work on yourself so that you have a solid structure on which to build everything else. The fourth Pillar – Integration – is where we focus on strategies, tools, tips and techniques that will create a new way of working that will help you to stop procrastinating and start to make the very most out of each and every day. Finally, the fifth Pillar – Tracking – is designed to make sure that you build everything you have learned into your life so you never have to go on another time management course ever again.

So, what can we do to make sure that we maximise our time on earth?

I am going to get this out of the way right up front so that it is stuck in your mind with every word that you read.

CONSISTENCY is the secret sauce that you need to spread over everything you do, and this will change your world forever. It is the key to everything and I cannot stress it enough. There are no prizes for dabblers. All of the prizes go to the people who can make consistency over everything they do as exciting as their first kiss!

Consistency trumps everything!
(Carl Pate)

Time is the only thing that everyone on earth has in common; there is no getting around it. We all have 24 hours in a day and 168 hours in a week and unless you are going to create your own planet, you just need to accept this. Time is the great and only leveller of all people. The difference between those who achieve the greatest successes and those who go to their death beds full of regrets about what might have been is how they use their time. This whole book is about that very principle and everything in here is designed to help you get a slight edge on where you are today. A series of small improvements will cumulate towards a lifestyle greater than you could ever imagine.

I am now well into my fiftieth year on this planet and about two years ago I decided to change direction completely. You may call it a mid-life crisis, but I call it a realisation that I could not afford to waste one more minute doing something that did not make me feel great. I spent the first 27 years of my working life in finance, with 16 as CFO of a major clothing manufacturer. For 23 of those years, I loved my work. I then tolerated two years and hated the last two years. That was the point when I snapped and had to move on.

I never really knew what I wanted to do with my life when I was younger so following the path of Chartered Accountant seemed to be a pretty safe bet, and that really meant something to me at the time. The problem was that this takes years of study and by the time I was 24 years old and a qualified Chartered Accountant, I was sick to death of studying and taking exams. I swore to myself that I would never study or take another exam for the rest of my life. And for ten years I held true to that promise.

Then one morning I got up and went downstairs to let the dogs out. While they were playing in the garden I switched on the TV. As I flicked through the channels I came across an infomercial for Get The Edge, a CD set by Tony Robbins. As I watched, it ignited something inside me, but I was damned if I was going to spend £120 on a set of CDs. Who does that, right? But it did interest me, so I went out and bought a single CD by Tony called Awaken the Giant Within. I listened to this over and over again and then decided to buy the Get The Edge CDs, still convinced that I would only need to listen to them once and would then send them back. I was pretty cheap back then and could not bear the idea of spending £120. Anyway, I bought the CDs and listened to them so many times that I think they are worn out now. They were never returned. Not only that, but £120 turned out to be a 'piss in a very enormous ocean', as I went on to attend all of Tony's live events at least twice, along with many other programmes. This was truly life changing.

The thing was, I had missed learning. And when I found it again [illegible] y life. This time I was not studying for exams, I was [illegible] to improve myself, and it felt great. However, there was [illegible] blem, I was becoming a seminar junkie! I was going to seminar after seminar, spending a fortune, getting really hyped up during the course and then hitting the ground with a thud when I got back home and life took over again. The truth was, I was learning a lot but I was not implementing anything. And learning without implementation is a complete waste of time.

So I spoke to my coach at the time, a lady called Karen Vice, who I will always credit with starting me off on the path of turning my learning into life changing strategies, and ultimately into the business that I created and still run today. Karen told me to get a sheet of paper and make a note of two things in each area of my life that, if performed every day, would support me and really make a difference, put this on the fridge and then tick them off day by day. Being the true Accountant that I was, rather than a sheet of paper I chose to create a spreadsheet which I used religiously, and that would later develop into my unique software, Daily Life Tracker ®, which I still use every single day to get incredible results.

This was the thing that changed it all. Instead of spending money on seminars, I was investing money in me and not only did it feel so much better, but I started getting the results I was looking for.

So, what was happening?

When I look back on those early seminars and ask myself what I was looking for, it is very clear that I was looking for the big bang or the magic bullet that would change my life in an instant. But following Karen's intervention, and the subsequent results that I started to achieve, I had this blinding realisation that the big bangs and magic bullets were an illusion. The truly life changing results would all come from simple actions performed consistently over time.

Introduction

Trust me, if you are looking for magic bullets you will only ever find magic bullshit! And there are plenty of people out there selling that if you really want it.

Extraordinary results can be achieved by mastering the BASICS. If you work on this, everything else will follow.

Ordinary activities consistently performed produce extraordinary results.
(Keith Cunningham)

We've all heard the phrase 'don't sweat the small stuff' coming from some well-meaning individual who wants to impress you with how important he is. Well, I say NONSENSE! It's all about the small stuff. Don't get me wrong, I'm not saying that you should worry about missing five minutes of your favourite soap or the dog chewing one of your slippers, what I mean is that all progress comes from simple actions. In this book we are going to look at those ordinary activities and see how we can use them to master and change our lives.

Everything that anyone has ever achieved has come from simple activities ACTIONED one step at a time. We cannot go from where we are today to a completely different place overnight. But one action today followed by another action and another, and all of a sudden our path has changed direction. And consequently, our destination will be a completely different place as long as we continue to follow through on these actions in a consistent and dynamic manner. Although you may not notice them happening when you are in the middle of your day because you are not paying attention, be absolutely sure that those small habits and rituals that you are building are establishing themselves within your very being. But beware, this same principle applies to bad habits as well as good.

Success is a few simple disciplines, practiced every day; while failure is simply a few errors in judgement, repeated every day.
(Jim Rohn)

This is what is known as the 'aggregation of marginal gains'. The principle is that by paying attention to the detail, a one degree shift in the right direction across multiple areas of your life supported by daily routines will cumulate over time into massive improvements. Equally, a one degree shift in the wrong direction will culminate in disaster. There are some obvious things that you can get started on, such as some daily movement like a walk or jog to start making progress towards a healthier body. But then there are less obvious things; things which in themselves probably make little difference to your life, and this might include flossing your teeth every night or making sure that as soon as a light bulb goes out in the house you replace it. What is happening here is that you are raising your standards, little by little every day, and whilst it appears that nothing has changed in your life as a result, these small things will cumulate into a person who has high standards in everything they do. Standards follow standards. When you raise your standards in one area of your life, other things start to improve as well, and conversely when you start to let your standards slip in one area, so goes everything else.

How you do anything, is how you do everything.
(T Harv Eker)

It is this one degree principle that I believe needs to be applied to every area of your life, and with this will come all the results and rewards that you desire. But it doesn't happen overnight. Tony Robbins says that "all change happens in an instant" and that "the time is taken in getting to the instant where you are ready to make the change". I understand that, and I actually believe it, but the problem is that changing for the moment is not the answer. The change needs to be consistent and long lasting, and this does take time. There will be tough times and there will be times when it is easy. The defining moments are the tough times. When it's easy, it's easy. But you have to push through the difficulties and the results will appear.

Raise your standards to a level that no-one else could ever expect of you.
(Michael Johnson)

The Japanese have long applied the art of Kaisan in their businesses. This is the application of continuous improvements, large and small, which cumulate into a strong and sustainable business. I like to think of the principles that I talk about in this book as personal Kaisan where the simple improvements applied and sustained day by day result in the best possible you!

Darren Hardy wrote a fabulous book called The Compound Effect. In fact, as I was reading it I thought he had been looking over my shoulder! The compound effect is all about layering one thing on top of another. The one degree principle only works if you are adding a new improvement onto the previous day's progress. Otherwise you are just a busy fool, improving random things by one degree and then going back to where you started. The real trick is that you must follow through with every improvement and consistently maintain it while building new growth into your life. For me, this is where Daily Life Tracker ® comes into its own. The system is very specifically designed to help in this area and you can see a much more detailed account of how we do this later in the book, in Pillar 5 – Tracking.

The issue most people have is that they do not stay the course. They dabble in this and that, but never actually stick with anything long enough for them to master it. One of my favourite quotes came from one of my favourite mentors, Keith Cunningham, who said, "Get in line, stay in line!". Keith explained how people treated life like a cafeteria line. They would start to get hungry and so they would join the end of the line. But the line would move much too slowly and they would get bored. They would see a shiny penny and get out of line to play for a while, and then realise they were still hungry. Unfortunately, the line would now be much longer and they would have to join at the back again, until they got bored once more and saw their next distraction. And so it goes on, they keep getting in line but never wait long enough to eat.

Get in line, stay in line!

(Keith Cunningham)

The power of compounding is undeniable. But it also takes time. At first very little appears to be happening, but over time a little bit of momentum starts to build. Then, as you continue to consistently apply the rules, all of a sudden the growth starts to take off exponentially. This is most easily demonstrated in financial terms. If, for example, you invest as little as £100 per month at a 12% annual return, your results over time are staggering as you can see in the table below:

Time	**Value**	**Time**	**Value**
5 years	£8,167	30 years	£349,496
10 years	£23,004	35 years	£643,096
15 years	£49,958	40 years	£1,176,477
20 years	£98,926	45 years	£2,145,469
25 years	£187,885	50 years	£3,905,864

Particularly look at the growth in the last three periods. After 50 years you are sitting on £3.9m having invested only £60,000 from your income over that period.

The principles of the compounding effect apply equally to all areas of your life. When you start to build a new skill, the work seems to have little impact. Then you start to see some glimmers of improvement that suddenly culminate in exponential development that turns you into an expert in your field.

Compound interest is the eighth wonder of the world. He who understands it, earns it.... he who doesn't .... pays it.
Compound interest is the most powerful force in the universe.
Compound interest is the greatest mathematical discovery of all time.
(Albert Einstein)

The big issue is that people are often too short term in their thinking. We are looking for instant gratification and to get away from this requires a shift in mindset.

It is your mindset that governs your actions, which lead to your results. If your mindset limits your potential, you will likely accept limited results in your life.

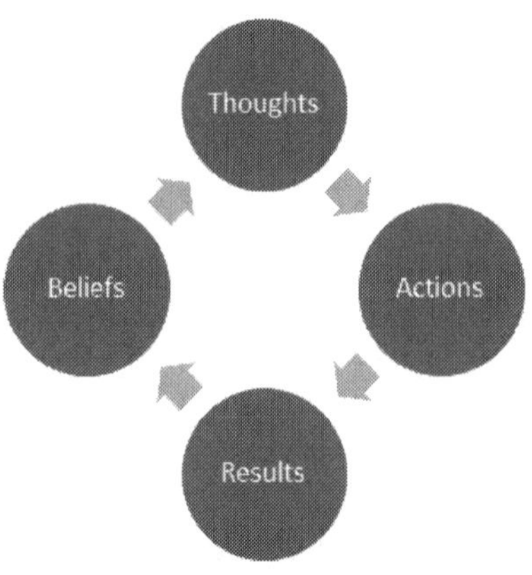

Results Cycle

Beware your thoughts for they become words
Beware your words for they become actions
Beware your actions for they become habits
Beware your habits for they form your character
Beware your character for this creates your destiny.
(Unknown)

Now, you might be thinking that you are a little impatient for all this 'ordinary activity' stuff and you want things much faster than that. There is nothing wrong with thinking like this. I have exactly the same thoughts. But nothing says that these small changes can't have a big impact. You just need to ignite a spark to start you moving in a new direction and then maintain its momentum. And the easiest way to do this is to change the identity that you hold for yourself. Ask yourself who is the person you want to become? Define that person very clearly. Use role models to help you. Define in detail who you want to be. How would that person eat, exercise, get up in the morning, be with the kids? How would they live their life? Then set out a plan of all the small changes you can make today to move you in that direction.

The trouble with the future is that it comes one day at a time.
(Unknown)

You can always up the pace.

I have long believed in practicing the art of simple activities consistently performed over time to get great results, so then I got thinking. If the compound effect works so well for small actions, how would it work on bigger, still consistent, actions. And this is when I decided to quit my job and get busy every day – writing, reading, learning and creating 12 to 18 hours per day. Could I accelerate the impact of the compound effect and condense what may take three years into one? And the answer is, of course, yes. The challenge is that you must remain CONSISTENT. If you are ready, lay down your plan and go for it.

Introduction

The starting point to this whole book can be found within this riddle. Read it, think about it, and don't turn the page until you have had a guess at the answer!

I am your constant companion.
I am your greatest helper and heaviest burden.
I will push you onward or drag you down to failure.
I am completely at your command.
Half the things you do you might just as well turn over to me
And I will be able to do them quickly and correctly. I am easily
managed, you just have to be firm with me.
Show me exactly how you want something to be done
And after just a few lessons I will do it automatically.
I am the servant of all great people
And, alas, of all failures, too.
Those who are great, I have made great.
Those who are failures, I have made failures.
I am not a machine, although I operate with all the precision of a
machine
Plus the intelligence of a human being.
You may run me for a profit or turn me to ruin
It makes no difference to me.
Take me, train me, be firm with me,
And I will place the world at your feet.
Be easy with me and I will destroy you.

Who am I?

I AM HABIT!

(Anonymous/The 8th Habit by Stephen R. Covey)

Pillar 1 – HABITS

Pillar 1 – HABITS

Your habits are the compounding of the mind.

(Carl Pate)

You have just read about the power of the compound effect and what Albert Einstein thinks about compound interest. So, if your habits are the compounding of the mind, how important do you think they are?

The dictionary defines habit as 'an acquired behaviour pattern, regularly followed until it has become almost involuntary'.

The real purpose to understanding habits is so we can change the ones we don't like and create ones that empower us.

In understanding your habits there are two critical questions you need to ask:

1) What makes you do the habit?

2) What will make you stop doing the habit?

In this Pillar, I will first explain exactly why we perform the habits we do and then at the end of the Pillar I will offer you a model that I call the 5 Ws of Transformation which will give you the power to change any habit faster than you ever dreamt possible.

Human beings don't like to think! Thinking is hard work. People are much more comfortable when they are working on autopilot and have created habits and routines. Getting to grips with new things is quite mentally draining because we have to think about them so much. The focused attention required to master anything new is so intense that we strive to automate as much as possible and create new habits. We need to drown out much of what is irrelevant noise.

Think about how it feels when you get a new phone, or when you were learning to drive. There is so much to think about at first, but when you have been doing it for a while the whole process gets moved onto autopilot – we get comfortable, feel less stressed and even take it for granted.

From the moment we get up to the moment we go to bed so much of what we do is driven by habit. Are you an alarm snoozer, or do you spring straight out of bed? Do you exercise first thing in the morning or check Facebook? Which leg do you dry first after you shower? Or is it a bath? Which route do you take to work? What is the first thing you do when you get into the office? Habit, Habit, Habit!

Our lives are engrained with habits and rituals. We all have them – some good, some bad, some neutral. But most of these are created by the world around us – the media or our work environment, for example. It is a strange fact of life that bad habits are created without any effort or attention, but good habits need to be cultivated on a consistent basis. Maybe it is God's way of ensuring we grow and become more.

How would it feel to know that your habits are working for you rather than against you? Every good habit affects everything else in your life. When you engage in a good habit your standards start to rise in many other areas of your life. But BEWARE… all those bad habits have a dramatic impact on everything else too… and this can lead to devastating consequences unless you ACT NOW and take charge.

We are what we repeatedly do. Excellence is not an act but a HABIT.
(Aristotle)

Everyone wants to change some of their habits. In fact, whenever anyone says that they want to change something, it is almost always some form of habit.

Researchers at Duke University suggested that 40% of what we do on a daily basis is not based on decisions we consciously make, but on habit. In my view, it is probably well in excess of 60%. In fact, the National Science Foundation suggests that we have around 50,000 thoughts every day and, rather disturbingly, 95% of those thoughts are repeated, reflecting the beliefs and values that we hold as true. No wonder so much of our lives are driven by habit.

If, [when I wake up in the morning,] I create my day and build small habits day by day, I start to notice – little by little – that my world is changing. Things that I found hard are getting easier. Indeed I notice new habits starting to build. This gives me the power and the incentive to do it again the next day, and the next day.
(Joe Dispenza, What the Bleep Do We Know!?)

When I was a child, one of my best teachers was Mr Frost, my Chemistry A-Level teacher. Better than anyone I know he knew the power of compounding the information in your mind so you did not have to cram for your exams at the end of the year. He had a simple process and it started on the second day of a two year syllabus. He took the first ten minutes of every lesson to randomly test us on what we had learned in the previous lessons. At first there was not too much to test, but as the months went by we could be asked questions on any topic and as a result we were always on top of the whole subject. Whilst this could be quite a pain, by the time I got to sit my A-Levels I did not have to revise this subject at all and I achieved a top grade A. This came from a ten minute repetition exercise which meant that I actually learned the subject properly. My own children are now working towards their GCSEs and I am trying to get them to heed this lesson. That is not easy to teach to a teenager, but it does work. The power of small increments is incredible.

The Habit Chain

Habits are driven by a four step habit chain as asserted by Charles Duhigg in his excellent book, The Power of Habit.

The Habit Chain

A habit is formed by repetition of an action over time, which strengthens connections in your brain to make the performance of that habit automatic. However, whatever habits we do have, we are not doing them all the time. So what makes us perform a habit? This is where the four step habit chain comes in. Something will act as a trigger which fires off the connections or pathways in your brain reminding you of the pleasure you receive from performing a particular routine. These neural pathways are strengthened by repetition and the more you repeat the habit, the stronger the pathway becomes.

Think of these pathways in your brain as threads of yarn. For each repetition another thread is added and interwoven into the last. After the first couple of threads are woven, the pathway will be relatively weak and easily broken, but once you have added five, ten, fifteen strands it starts to get stronger and much harder to break. After years of unconsciously performing these habits you have so many threads of yarn that the links become as strong as a rope.

The other critical thing to bear in mind here is emotion. The more powerful your emotions at the time of triggering the habit chain, the stronger will be the thread created by this single episode. This means that fewer repetitions of the habit will create greater strength in the pathway. This explains why some habits can be created very quickly while others take a lot longer to form. Eventually, after a number of repetitions this habit chain becomes automatic, driven by your powerful subconscious mind, and you feel powerless to change it.

But you are not powerless. Especially if you understand the breakdown of the habit pattern. Rather counterintuitively, the routine itself is almost a side issue. The formation of the habit, or pathway in the brain, is driven emotionally between the trigger and the desire for the pleasure you get at the end of the process. Willpower alone will not change a habit in the long run because the pathway in the brain will always exist. As long as the trigger also continues to exist, your conscious mind will always be in a fight with your subconscious mind, and this is a lot of hard work.

Once you have the understanding of how your brain works to create your habit patterns, you can work on the individual steps within that routine, allowing a much easier change process. In fact, now you understand the subconscious steps that your brain goes through in creating your habits, you can use that very process to override them.

The Role of Focus in the Habit Chain

Whilst a simple trigger starts the process, there is a gap between the trigger and the routine, and it is within this gap that we can refocus our minds and interrupt the pattern. Sometimes this gap is almost imperceptible and you automatically perform the routine without even noticing what happened. At other times, there can be an extended period between the trigger and the response, although you are still very drawn to the old pattern. What has happened here is that the trigger has reminded you of the potential for a pleasurable experience but in order for you to get that pleasurable experience you need to actually make a decision to perform the routine that you know gives you the pleasure. This gap, between stimulus and response, gives you the opportunity to make a choice – do you do it and add another thread of yarn to the habit chain or do you stop yourself and weaken those links. If at the time of the trigger, you are able to soften or redirect that focus then you have the opportunity to stop the routine or even the desire for the pleasure. But this is a choice that you need to make. The mere awareness that you have gained by studying this process gives you an incredible advantage over everyone else because you now recognise that it is a choice and not just an inevitable progression.

One problem with this is that if you make the choice not to perform that routine then your brain can get very focused on what it is missing out on. Your brain can be very cunning and try all sorts of tricks to get you to follow the old pattern because it knows that by doing this you will certainly receive the pleasure that it so desires. So you need to outsmart your brain. Your job here is to teach your instincts that there are other more empowering routes to that same pleasure sensation. Later in this Pillar, we will look into what I call the 5 Ws of Transformation which provide a practical way around this problem.

At this stage, we need to move on to examine the final part of the process – the pleasure we gain from performing the habit, or the reward. This pleasure can be anything ranging from a taste sensation you get from eating a bar of chocolate to the feeling of pride and accomplishment you get from completing your daily exercise routine or recording your achievements in a daily log.

Alpha Needs

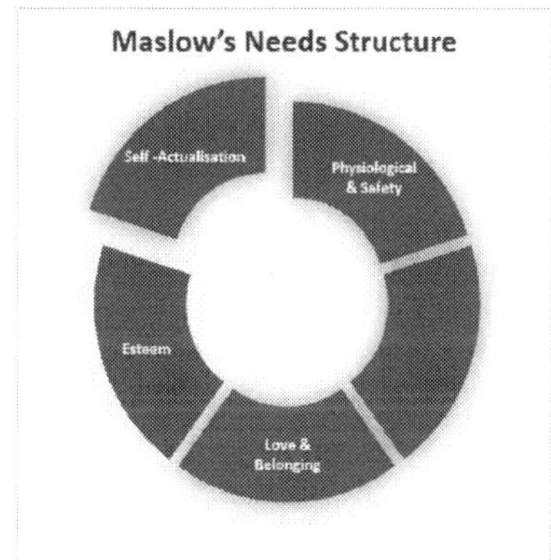

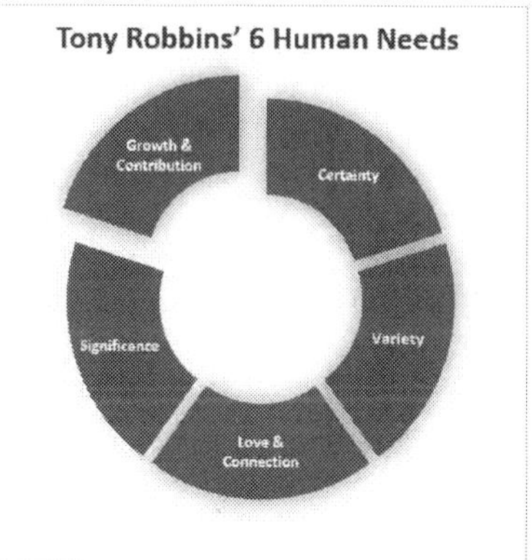

Human Needs Structure

Originally developed to explain and resolve conflict, human needs psychology has morphed into a more mainstream model explaining why human beings do what they do. And whatever we as human beings do, we do for a reason and that reason is to meet our needs. There has been much written about human needs, from Abraham Maslow to Tony Robbins and many others in between. This work is really the key to understanding why habits become so engrained within our lives. Even though you will read this part of the book in about five minutes, I suggest you stop and take in what is being said here as the understanding of this is profound and will change your life. Take some time to go online and study it.

The basic principle is that all human beings, no matter what their background or where they come from, share a needs structure that evidences itself in everything they do and feel. We all have different methods of satisfying these needs, but satisfy them we will. According to Tony Robbins take on this subject, there are six human needs. The first four needs are the needs of the personality and everyone must meet these needs, and they will meet them whether in good ways or bad. The last two needs, the need for growth and contribution, are more spiritual needs, which Maslow referred to as self-actualisation, and it is the meeting of these needs that creates the greatest fulfilment in our lives.

Certainty

This is the most basic of all of our needs as it relates to our survival. Everyone needs to feel that they are in control and that they have some say over where their life is going. Fear stems from a need for certainty yet, according to Tony Robbins, the quality of our life is directly proportional to the amount of uncertainty we can comfortably cope with. When our certainty is taken away, nothing else matters and you will do everything you can to regain it.

Variety

If everything is too certain, you get bored. We all love a nice surprise and it is this variety that creates the spice in our lives. Interestingly, the need for variety is in conflict with our need for certainty. Balancing these two needs is part of the rich joy of life.

The quality of our lives is directly proportional to the amount of uncertainty that we can comfortably deal with.

(Tony Robbins)

Significance

Everyone craves the feeling that what we do or who we are matters and that our lives have meaning. Significance is the feeling of power and self-worth that we all need.

Love and Connection

We all need to feel like we belong and that we have someone to love and who loves us. This is fairly self-explanatory, although it does create a paradox with the third need for significance since if we are too special and significant then no-one can relate to us.

Growth

It is a truism of life that we must grow and become more than we currently are. If you are not growing, you are dying; there is no in-between. There is no sadder reflection on human life than seeing someone who has given up on expanding themselves. On the other hand, when Michael Johnson was asked about the secret to his success he said that "you must raise your standards to a level that no-one else could ever expect of you". When you take this approach to everything you do, you unconsciously give everyone around you permission to do the same.

Contribution

And finally, we have the need to contribute beyond ourselves and give back to the world and those with whom we share it. Whether this be to our families, our community or to the whole of society and the world around us, we have an innate need to leave the world in a better place than when we found it.

The way we go about meeting our needs will determine the quality of our lives.

The Interaction of Habits and Needs

A habit will only continue if we gain some pleasure at the end of it. If you understand what need a habit is meeting, you are in a great place to move to the next step to change it.

It is important to understand that you cannot stop a bad habit. You can only replace it with a different one. Simply trying to quit a habit just leaves a vacuum in the pathway of your brain and basic physics tells us that without a lot of hard work and effort, this vacuum will get filled. The most likely thing to fill it is the old habit since that was already part of the initial habit chain. This is why diets don't work and why people, more often than not, fail at New Year's resolutions, or indeed at changing habits at any time of the year. In order to avoid this, therefore, we must replace the habit with an empowering alternative.

If you are having trouble giving something up, and have had this problem for a long time, try putting the elimination goal to one side and create a new empowering habit that simply replaces the old one. This may seem like a subtle difference, but it is a powerful one.

If the habit you are trying to change is meeting four of your needs at level 7 to 9 (on a scale of 1 to 10) then your replacement habit must also meet these same needs at least at the same level. If you try to replace a habit that satisfies your need for certainty and significance with one that only meets your need for variety then this will not work in the long run because the vacuum within your need for certainty and significance still exists and the old habit is likely to return to replace it. Equally, if you replace a habit with something that meets your needs at a lower level, you will not get the same satisfaction from the new habit and this is also doomed to failure. We, therefore, need to carefully create new habit routines which give you equal or greater pleasure than the old ones.

By way of an example, let's say that when you're feeling under pressure your go-to response is to shout in order to get everyone to comply with your wishes. The primary needs this response is meeting are certainty and significance. In this example, you are meeting the need for certainty at level 8 (out of 10) which is a high result as, judging from past experience, when you start to yell, people do what you say. You also meet the need for significance at level 8 because shouting makes you feel powerful, although this is probably more of a perceived level in your own mind as the people around you probably don't see it that way at all. However, critical here is how you perceive your needs being met rather than what anyone else thinks. You also meet your need for variety at level 5 as you don't know what people's reaction is going to be and that adds an extra element of interest. The other needs are met at much lower levels. You can see below how we may represent this in a chart, which demonstrates how meeting your needs for certainty and significance may result in this turning into a habit.

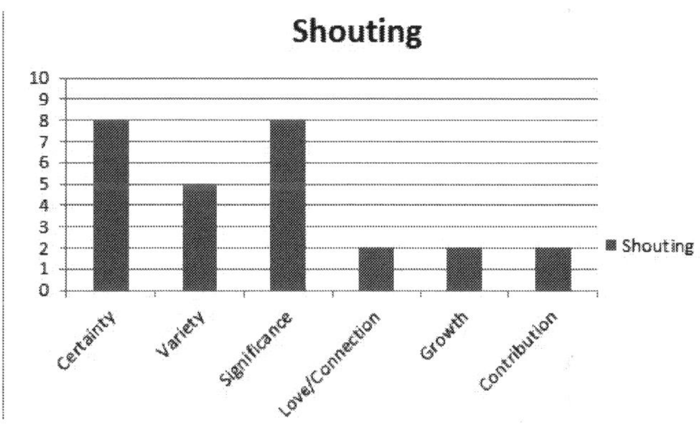

Let's say you now decide that this is not really working for you and you want to take a different approach. You decide that instead of yelling at everyone to get your own way, you are now going to try to bring them on side by joking around. This way, you feel they will have more sympathy with you and will therefore comply with your wishes. You can see from the chart below that this theory is flawed as it may well raise your need for variety to level 8 but you never quite know how it is going to go, which reduces your need for certainty down to level 3, and it is a pretty hollow approach when you do it all of the time, reducing your feelings of significance to level 3. Trying to plug the gap with this approach will not work as your key needs for certainty and significance are not at all satisfied.

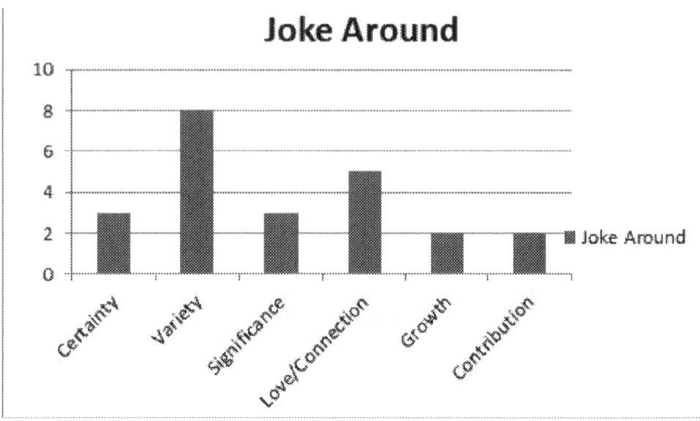

By way of contrast, if you decide that your new approach is to create teams of people and involve them in key discussions, you can easily see (as shown in the chart below) that this is a great replacement for your previous habit of shouting. Not only are your needs for certainty and significance met at higher levels than they were before, but all your other needs are also met at considerably higher levels. It is easy to see how, with a few focused repetitions of this practice, a new much more empowering and satisfying habit can be formed.

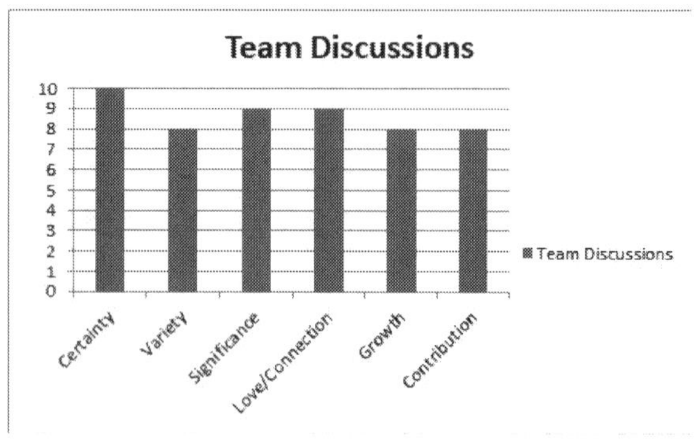

Incidentally, according to Tony Robbins' work on this subject, if you meet just two of these needs at a high level of 7 or above, you will form a habit, and if you meet at least four of your needs at level 7 and over, you are likely to have created an addiction.

Spotting a Bad Habit

It is easy to start a bad habit, and we all know that this leads to yet more bad habits. And if this passes unnoticed, it can lead to devastation over time. It is like the old adage of putting the frog in boiling water. If you drop him into the boiling water, he will jump straight out, but if you put him in cold water and slowly heat it up, he will boil to death. Without instant feedback on how you are doing, you will be like the frog slowly and unwittingly moving towards disaster.

Two Types of Bad Habit

It seems to me that there are two types of bad habit that we want to do something about, and we have separate ultimate goals for each one. The first type of bad habit is the one we NEVER want to do ever again which would include things like taking drugs or smoking. The second type of bad habit is not quite so significant, but is a habit that we recognise has started to take control over our lives, rather than the other way around. The goal here is to bring this habit under control so you are making proper choices rather than simply sleepwalking into this routine. Examples of this type of habit might be eating chocolate or drinking alcohol.

So what is the difference? The distinction between the first and second categories may be clear in some instances. I would hope that no-one who is reading this book thinks that doing drugs is OK once in a while, but depending on your background and point of view some people will put drinking alcohol and smoking into the 'never ever' category and some will believe that it is OK on special occasions or even once a week. The distinction between the categories is a personal choice. But once we have decided in which category these habits lie, we need to address them in different ways.

The problem you have, if you are working on a habit that you simply want to get under control arises from the question as to whether you have actually broken the chain and you are now simply performing a random action that has no control over you or have you re-established the chain, pushing yourself back into the habit and moving yourself back to where you started from.

On the one hand, this seems like another one of those tricks your brain is playing on you to get you back into the habit and bring it the pleasure it so desires. On the other hand, the real goal in this instance is to put yourself in control of the habit rather than the other way around. You, therefore, need to test it otherwise you are accepting that this was a habit that has the upper hand over you. And sometimes we need to be a little flexible in the things we do so we can experience all of the joys of life.

If, when you test this habit, you find that you can never do this thing again, even once, without re-establishing the old pattern, then you have determined that the habit controls you and not you the habit.

If we examine bad habits a little further for a moment, there are two extremes to the process – one extreme is that you cannot stop doing the habit and the other extreme is that you have stopped and you can never do this routine again otherwise you risk recreating the old habit. This is two sides of the same coin – the habit has control over you one way or the other, although obviously resisting the habit serves you much better.

The goal with your habits is always to bring them within your control so they do not affect you.

Killer of Progress

One of the biggest killers of progress in your life lies in your inability to change your habits. We saw in the riddle at the beginning of the book that Habit is the servant of everyone – success or failure – and the difference between the two is simply your ability to become the master of your habits.

Beware Your Subconscious Mind

When you start trying to take control of your bad habits your internal enemy is going to show up and start trying to persuade you to quit. You need to be constantly on your guard for the tell-tale phrases that tell you your subconscious mind is trying to sabotage your progress. These phrases include, but are not limited to:

- "Just this once."
- "This is the last time."
- "Everyone else does it."
- "No-one will know."
- "I'm going to treat myself."
- "What the hell, I've had a bad day. I'll get back to it tomorrow."

Stand guard at the door of your mind.
(Jim Rohn)

These are backward steps, and although it may seem insignificant to veer off track for one time, this is a dangerous game. Every time you let this happen you strengthen the bad habit and you weaken your new habit, but more importantly you weaken your resolve and your power and belief that you have this under control.

I have even found myself recognising that this is my subconscious mind tricking me with the 'just this once' promise, but then twisting it to say "OK, I know what you are doing, so I am going to come off track this one time to prove to you that I am actually in control and I can just do it this once." NO! You cannot let this happen. This is another brain trick trying to manipulate you again.

One of the biggest problems I have found is getting past that feeling of NEVER being able to do something ever again. This habit you are trying to change, after all, served you in the past and helped you meet your needs. When you force yourself to never do something you have previously enjoyed, you are creating a scarcity within your mind. This scarcity plagues your mind and keeps you focusing on the thing you want to stop doing. And whatever you focus on you get drawn towards, so you create a vicious cycle.

To get beyond this psychological problem, it is indeed advisable, especially in the early stages of transformation, to allow yourself one or two days' grace. This removes the scarcity trap that can pull you back in because you cannot face the possibility of never eating chocolate again!

The issue lies in where control resides. Are you in control and this was a planned departure from your new habit? Or is your subconscious mind trying to trick you back into your old ways?

When you find yourself in this position (and you will) you need to remind yourself of the reasons you want to give up this habit (see the 5 Ws of Transformation). And then remind yourself that all you need to do is stop this one time, in this moment. Tell yourself it is not forever as you have a day off planned later in the week. If you can do this, your strength, resolve and belief in the process and your ability to operate that process will build and the neural links forming the old habit will weaken.

There is an added bonus to stopping yourself going off track – it starts to change the identity you have for yourself. You start to see yourself as someone who is in control and who can do anything. When you defeat a bad habit, other habits follow, like when you avoid buying a bar of chocolate every time you go to the service station and all of a sudden you find yourself not biting your nails. Not because you had been trying, but because you are now not the sort of person who does that.

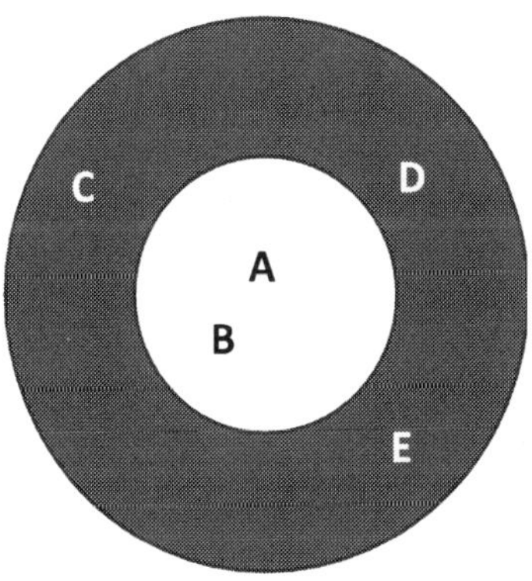

The Habit Zone

If A and B represent habits you are already in control of and you now expand your control over habit C, you can also find yourself able to master habits D and E as your experience of your capabilities grows.

But remember, you are doing it one day at a time – just stop this once. Don't tell yourself that it is forever because the scarcity of this may tempt you back. The next time you are tempted, avoid it that one time and then the next time and then the next time. All the time, with each break of the habit, you are building your identity as someone in control and who does not do these things. You know your brain better than anyone else, so figure out how to outsmart it.

Change is achieved step by step, day by day, which makes any change simple and doable. However, the simple fact that this is so easy is also the reason most people fail to achieve the changes they want to achieve. If you are looking to stop doing something, it is pretty easy to not do it the next time. We can all put that piece of chocolate down this once. However, this very fact is what makes it so easy to continue with the old habit, just this once. Just doing it one more time won't make any difference, will it? WRONG! This makes all the difference. You are trying to unwind a rope's worth of individual threads of yarn built up over many years – when you perform the old habit, even just this once, you are stopping this reversal process and restrengthening the old habit. And if you do stop the habit this one time, this provides an added psychological benefit.

The linkage of neuro-connections is actually strengthened by your awareness that you were trying to stop but did not manage it. This tells your brain that this stuff does not work. Whereas if you do actually stop, this starts to tell your brain that this process does actually work and you build psychological strength so you are more likely not to do the habit the next time round.

The problem is that even if we now have the skills to change the habit very quickly, we still get impatient for the results. Persistence is the key. You did not get fat overnight and you cannot expect to get thin overnight either.

I remember reading somewhere about a test that Warren Buffett likes to do to see if he is acting with integrity. It goes something like this: 'If a reputable journalist working for a world-class newspaper were to follow your every move and report on you every day in a fair and unbiased way, would you be happy for your friends, family, colleagues and clients to read what he wrote?' If the answer is no, then you know what you need to do.

Transformation of a Habit

Now that we understand how habits work, and how to effectively replace them, we need to move back to the initial trigger for the habit. To break the habit we must interrupt the pattern that is creating it at exactly the right time. After all, we have already said that these habits happen automatically within our subconscious mind. By being aware of the habit and its various components and giving some thought to the trigger that usually sets off this habit, you can be ready with a system to stop the habit before it occurs.

First, you need to know what buttons to press in your mind as this will give you the drive to change. What is it that really matters to you that will make you want to change – is it family, the need for growth, the need for power? When you see the trigger approaching (and awareness will help here), you can remind yourself of what you are changing and what the new process will be. This will be tricky at first as habits by their nature are very engrained in your life, but if you're prepared and ready for the trigger, you can interrupt the pattern at exactly the right moment.

Interrupting the pattern is key to breaking a habit and the more outrageous your method of breaking the pattern, the more likely you are to make it work. As you interrupt the pattern, you can then slot in the new routine. Sometimes it can be hard to remember to do this when you are actually in the throes of the habit, so what you can do to help the process is imagine very vividly yourself being in that situation – imagine the trigger, crush the old habit in your mind and slide the new habit elegantly into place, leaving the old reward at the end. Do this several times and the new habit will start to embed itself even before you come across the real situation. After all, your brain does not know the difference between reality and your imagination.

One critical feature here is to be aware of the circumstances of the trigger. For example, if the trigger to your habit is being alone and, say, every time you are alone you go to the kitchen and grab something unhealthy to snack on, you cannot create a new replacement habit that has you working out with a friend, for example. Whilst the latter might be a great new habit to create, in this instance it is inconsistent with the trigger, which is being alone. To replace this habit, which has a trigger of aloneness, you must replace it with a habit that you can do alone. After all, there are always going to be times when you are alone and you need to be ready with an appropriate replacement.

Once you are ready, you can make the changes you desire very quickly. You just need to get ready for that change, which may take a little longer. And this is not to be underestimated. To really make a change happen and stick with it, you need to be psychologically ready to go there. The 5 Ws model that follows is designed to help accelerate you towards that point of decision and then keep you on track.

Whatever changes you make to your habit patterns, you must be able to sustain them over time. Let's not sugar coat it, deeply engrained habits can be very difficult to change.

The 5 Ws of Transformation

There are, what I call, 5 Ws to all habit transformations. If you can master these principles, you can change any habit with ease and elegance. So here they are, in this order:

1. What
2. Why
3. When
4. Wish
5. Watch

It's rather like dialling a phone number, put the numbers in the wrong order and you will never get through.

Every element of the 5 Ws is important in the transformation process.

So, let's look at each of them in turn.

What?

They say that clarity is power.

Before you can change anything, you need to know precisely what it is you want to change. You need to define it as clearly as possible; firstly so you know what it is you are addressing and secondly so you know when you are done.

Be careful not to confuse habits and the results of those habits. Whilst the result may be that you are overweight, here you would need to clearly define the habits that have resulted in this situation, such as eating fast food and never exercising.

Why?

This is probably the most powerful and yet most overlooked piece of the jigsaw.

Why do you want to change?

Understanding why you want to change means understanding who you are and what drives you.

Most people immediately jump to thinking about how they are going to make the change, but this is actually a secondary matter. With a big enough 'Why', you reduce the need for willpower and have the power to do anything. With a big enough 'Why', you will always find a way to do something.

I am a big believer in goal setting, but the real power comes from the intensity of your desire. I do believe that we can achieve anything we want, but there is always a price to pay. It is only when you truly understand why you want something that you can determine whether you are willing to pay the price and make those sacrifices.

Whatever the mind can conceive and believe, it can achieve.
(Napoleon Hill)

Emotion plays a major role in moving you forward. If you can attach enough emotions to your reasons why you want to change you will undoubtedly achieve it.

Conversely, if you do not really know the emotional and powerful reason why you want to make the change then something else will always come along to distract you from your path.

The whole deal with habits is that they are firmly engrained within your brain and if you want to make a change it will take some effort. Having a big enough 'Why' to drive you towards your goal will short circuit a lot of this work. Through visualisation you can also make the consequences of your old habits much worse than they really are, thereby supercharging your reason why. By doing this, it increases the drive for change, but it is done in the confines and safety of your own mind.

A friend of mine, James, suggested that you list 75 powerful reasons why you want to change. With this level of commitment, it is hard to see how you can fail.

Alcoholics Anonymous is one of the most powerful and long established habit changing organisations in the world. One of the biggest factors in their success is that they insist that the people on their programme look for a higher purpose for the change manifested through their religious beliefs.

Whether your 'Why' is based in religion, a love for your family or the desire to change the world is for no-one other than you to decide, but you can be certain that the bigger your reasons, the easier will be the change process.

When?

Whilst habits form a significant part of our day, we are not always performing any specific individual habit. The process starts with the trigger, which is WHEN we need to be at our most aware. When the trigger goes off we need to be ready to intercept the process, and the trigger for the old habit now needs to fire off the new one.

One problem you will encounter is that the moment you need to intercept the pattern is the very moment you will not want to do it. Subconscious primal emotion will take over and your intellect will fall. To get around this, you need to visualise the situation in your mind before it happens. Your brain does not know the difference between reality and what you vividly imagine. Inside of this process you can interrupt the pattern and elegantly slide in an empowering replacement routine.

Wish

Having established the habit you want to change, what do you WISH to put in its place?

The starting point here would be to go back to your needs. We have already established that we perform our habits in order to gain a pleasure sensation and this pleasure sensation is the manifestation of us meeting one or more of our needs.

Therefore, the first thing to do is to establish which of our needs are being met in the performance of the original habit we want to change.

In order to effectively replace the old habit, you need to satisfy the same needs that were being met by the old habit within the new one. Not only that, but you need to meet these needs at least at the same level or better on a scale of 1 to 10.

Having established the more empowering habit you WISH for, this needs to become the focus of your attention as you will always move towards what you focus on.

I was once asked why I don't participate in anti-war demonstrations. I said that I will never do that, but as soon as you have a pro-peace rally, I'll be there.

(Mother Teresa, now Saint Teresa of Calcutta)

Remember, when you replace your old bad habit with a new empowering habit you must be consistent and congruent. Consistency means that the new habit must meet the same needs. Congruence means that you must be able to perform it in the same environment.

Watch

The final step in transforming any habit is to very carefully WATCH what is happening. By its nature a habit is a long engrained system within your brain that will continue to occur unless you make a conscious effort to change it. Getting in the way of a habit and stopping it once or twice by no account means that you have broken the habit. This requires a conditioning process that takes time. In order to make sure you continue on your desired path, you must continue to monitor your actions and measure your progress.

If you fall off the rails and start to perform your old habits again, this is not the end of the world, but if you want to produce lasting change you must make sure this is only a temporary occurrence and bring yourself back onto your new path.

Without self-discipline success is impossible.
(Lou Holtz)

If you do not know how to measure what you are looking to change then you have not given it enough thought. If you have not given it enough thought, you will not take the right actions at the right time. A small amount of thought up front will pay huge dividends in the long run as you master your new habit and move on to the next level.

Make It Worse Than It Is!

A friend of mine, Ricky, used to smoke like a chimney – 20 to 40 cigarettes a day for years. He smoked at home, in the car and, as often as not, you would see him lighting up outside the offices on a cigarette break. I don't think I have ever come across anyone who actually wants to smoke – this is one of those habits that pretty much everyone who does it wants to quit. So why don't they? And why didn't Ricky? When the habit gets a hold and links the neuro-connections within your brain, you are pretty much done for. Or are you? Of course not. We have talked about how we can change habits, but habits this deep and long standing can be really tough to break especially when the medics tell you that nicotine is addictive in a chemical way. This gives you the excuse not to even make an effort. After all, it's not your fault – it is the chemicals these tobacco companies put into their products that are to blame so it is really pointless trying. Let me tell you, the problem is not the chemicals, the problem is that you have not found a big enough reason to stop – a big enough WHY.

Let's go back to Ricky, a 20 to 40 cigarettes a day guy who occasionally, like everyone else, tries to stop but, let's face it, never really intends to. That is, until catastrophe strikes. One Monday morning, around February 2004, we get a call saying that Ricky is in intensive care and that he will not be in the office for some time. On Sunday evening, he started to feel ill and this rapidly went from an uncomfortable feeling to a desperate need to get to hospital. As he gets into the ambulance, the real drama starts. His breathing starts to get shallow and then it stops. The next 60 seconds are crucial in these circumstances and fortunately there happens to be a guy on board the ambulance who knows how to do a tracheotomy. Without any time to spare, he cuts a hole in Ricky's windpipe and inserts a tube into the opening to allow the air to get to his lungs. This was enough to get him to hospital where he could be treated and eventually progress to a full recovery.

Who knows, maybe this was always going to happen, but the smoking didn't help and was almost certainly a major contributing factor. And, what do you know? Ricky has never put a cigarette to his lips ever since. Why? Actually, it was not the obvious reason – because he nearly died. After all, Ricky is an intelligent guy and he had known all along that smoking was killing him, it was just never quite so immediate. Ricky's reason for never smoking again is because of how grateful he is to all the doctors and nurses and especially the paramedic whose quick actions meant that he could see his wife and daughter again, and later become a grandad. To pick up another cigarette would be a slap in the face to all those people who pulled him through the most critical of times. It is often only by looking outside of ourselves that we find our greatest strength. Now let's get clear here, this incident did not change Ricky's chemical make-up and make it easier than it was before to give up or easier than it is for anyone else. The ONLY thing that changed was that now he had a big enough reason to give up.

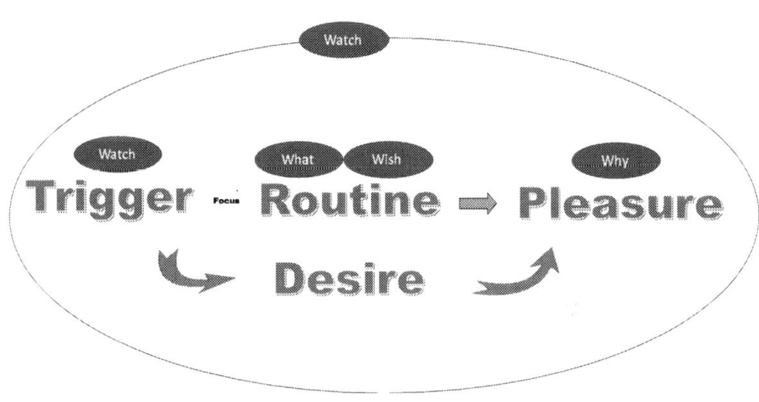

Habit Summary

The 5 Pillars in Action

Pick a habit you want to change and write out the 5 Ws that will get you there.

Habit:	
What	
Why	
When	
Wish	
Watch	

Pillar 2 –
ALIGNMENT

Pillar 2 – ALIGNMENT

Take Control of Your Life

I know that alignment is a bit of a buzz word and probably means something very specific in the world of social media and the likes, but for me alignment means working on yourself and taking control of your life. Alignment is focusing on yourself and practicing to improve. This is essentially personal development. The best definition of personal development I have found is: "Working to become the person that you want to be".

After racing through Heathrow Airport in what my family has come to lovingly refer to as 'Airport Dad' style, I am finally sitting comfortably in my seat ready to head off on one of our biannual trips to Houston, Texas to visit my wife's family. There are four of us – me, my wife Andrea, my son Phoenix and my daughter McKenzie. We have done the trip countless times over the last 13 years, but this time I decide to pay attention to the video instructions on what to do in case of an emergency. Just in case there are any non-humans on board, they tell us how to fasten and release our seat belts and then they let us know that our life jackets are under our seats. Then they instruct us on what to do in case of a sudden drop in cabin pressure. Oxygen masks will be released from above our heads and we should fit them over our nose and mouth and tighten with the rubber band. We are then instructed that if we are travelling with young children we should fit our mask first before helping our children with theirs. Now as a loving father in such dire circumstances, surely I should be helping my kids first before I start worrying about myself. After all, as parents we would do anything for our kids, even sacrifice our own lives for them. But the instruction is that I look after myself first, and only then worry about the kids. Why is this? The reason, of course, is that you need to be in full control of yourself and your own situation in order to be able to attend to anyone else effectively, no matter how important they are to you.

Give to yourself until your cup runneth over – and then give to others from the overflow.
(Iyanla Vanzant)

In reality, this is actually not a startling instruction to receive in an emergency situation on an aeroplane. We can all understand why. Even the most devoted parent gets it and is willing to follow this instruction.

However, this same principle, which should be applied in exactly the same way and for exactly the same reasons, with the rest of your life is completely missed by the majority of people. If you take a poll of almost any population and ask who their number one priority is in life, they will almost always come back with the answer that it is someone other than themselves, especially if they are married with children. Rarely would you find someone saying that they always take care of themselves first because this makes them look incredibly selfish. But the reality is that life is no different than the cabin pressure instructions on an aeroplane.

First and foremost, you must look after yourself. If you are not on top of your game, you cannot possibly give everything that you have to someone else. This applies to all areas of your life. For example, if you make one of your major priorities to look after your health, then you are not only healthy and vital enough to have the energy required to get out and change the world, but you also set an example for everyone around you to follow.

This even applies to your financial situation. Many people struggle with the concept of money. If you don't have it, it is the source of much discomfort and unhappiness. People with no money often look at those who do have it with some disdain and resentment. They see people with money as being greedy and selfish and often talk about how this money should be redistributed to the likes of themselves. But let's take a look at this through the lens of the aeroplane cabin pressure metaphor. If you have no money, at best the only person you can help is yourself. Once you have satisfied your own needs financially, only then can you start to help others in a meaningful way. First your close family, then perhaps your wider family and community and then the rest of the world.

This Pillar is all about focusing on YOU and getting everything aligned so all your efforts are working towards the same goal. It is about taking action and moving forwards. Sometimes this will terrify you but that is not a bad thing. All of your progress sits on the outside of your comfort zone. Inside your comfort zone is a life of mediocracy. It is time to step up and step out.

If everything seems under control, you're not going fast enough.
(Mario Andretti)

Energy

Before you read on, I want to stop you and make sure you really pay attention to this. Working on your energy levels is by far the biggest bang for your buck when it comes to improving your productivity and hence your time management. Everything else you want sits on the other side of getting your energy levels sorted out and in order. And yet, very few people who talk about time management spend any time on energy. So why do I make this bold assertion? Well, whatever you do with your energy levels, you take into the rest of your life. All the other strategies and techniques we talk about throughout this book will undoubtedly improve your personal productivity if you diligently apply them. But working on your energy levels has a global impact throughout the whole of your life and improves your productivity from the moment you get up until the moment you go to bed.

So how do we deal with this challenge? Well firstly, there are not a thousand things we have to worry about. There are only a handful, and the best approach is to experiment. Treat your body as a test lab and see what works for YOU. Don't go comparing yourself to everyone else because you are different and it will only serve to weaken you since you are going to do one of two things. Either you are going to compare yourself to other people who are in even worse shape than you so you feel better about yourself and do not get up and do anything about your situation or you are going to compare yourself to that friend who seems to be able to eat anything, never exercises and looks as skinny as a stick. In this case, you get depressed because they have it so easy and it must just be you, so again you do nothing about it other than fall deeper into despair.

So how do we stabilise our energy levels so we can get the sort of results we dream of?

Put simply, there are five elements that when taken care of will increase your energy levels dramatically:

1) How you move
2) What you put into your body
3) When you put it in
4) Building your strength
5) How you sleep

Now, of course, this oversimplifies things but it also starts to help you see that it is manageable.

The way to approach each of these principles is to first think about what makes common sense to you. Does it feel right to avoid carbs and sugars and go for a high fat and moderate protein diet? Does it feel right to drink a glass of wine every day? Does it feel right to exercise like crazy to the point of collapse or does it feel right to take a softer approach that you may stick to for longer? I am not here to answer these questions for you, only to pose them and get you thinking about what makes common sense to you.

Next, it would be a good idea to find a coach or mentor whose principles fit with your common sense approach. Coaches and mentors, or even friends who will hold you to account, are an invaluable resource in your efforts towards personal growth. But make sure that they are aligned with you. There is nothing worse than having an expert dragging you, kicking and screaming, towards something you do not believe in. You will never stick at it. And remember that whilst it would always be best to have a coach or mentor you can actually speak to, there are an enormous amount of online resources that can help and support you in this way and the best ones are set up to support you whatever your budget. You just get different levels of interaction.

How You Move

When it comes to exercise, don't go crazy. One piece of advice I would offer is that you should approach exercise in the following specific order:

1) Consistency
2) Duration
3) Intensity

This approach will help you to make sure that you build new lifelong habits.

You first need to select a level of exercise that you know you can consistently adhere to, even if it is simply to walk around the block for 15 minutes four nights a week. Once you start to consistently make these changes (see Habit Pillar for further support) you will start to feel good about yourself and want to do more.

This is when you need to increase the duration. Simply move to 30 minutes five nights a week for example, and then maybe to 45 minutes. The whole idea is that you are changing your lifestyle and so it has to be something you know you can do long term.

Finally, once you are happy that you are consistently taking more and more of the right actions, you can think about increasing the intensity. Now this might only be once or twice a week, but what you are going to do is push yourself a lot harder for half an hour or so while exercising. (If you are not used to this, please take professional and/or medical advice before taking this step.) Remember, nothing will make you quit faster than creating a regime that hurts.

What You Put Into Your Body and When You Put It In

Coming up with a detailed health programme is really beyond the scope of this book, but there are some basic concepts that if we get them right will give us boundless energy and if we get them wrong will bring us untold pain and suffering. In the world of personal development, I believe that so much has been written on the subject of health, energy and nutrition, and everything that goes with it, that it is one of the most confusing areas for people to navigate. There seems to be more different diets and exercise models than you could ever imagine. One person will eat no carbohydrates at all and achieve outstanding results and show you countless others who have done the same. Then someone else will tell you that they eat huge amounts of carbs and avoid fats like the plague and they seem to get the same outstanding results. They cannot all be right, can they? But they are, because they are getting the results. The problem for us as individuals is that we are all very different and we cannot assume that just because something works for one person it will also work for us. The one common factor I have found in all who get the best results from whichever diet they choose is that they are absolutely 100% consistent in what they do. They are not dabbling here and there with different plans. They are not confusing the matter with cheat days. They have a plan and they stick to it.

Whilst I am not going to lay out a detailed nutritional plan, what I will offer you, very briefly, is that the best way I have found to get these results is by applying a ketogenic lifestyle accompanied by intermittent fasting. I say lifestyle as I do not like to go on diets. The ketogenic lifestyle involves eating very low levels of carbohydrate (5% to 10%), moderate levels of protein (20%) and high levels of fat (70% to 75%).

Intermittent fasting merely involves refraining from eating for a 16 hour period. I choose to fast from 8pm one day until 12pm the following day. The thing is, science shows that after about ten to twelve hours of not eating, the glycogen levels in the liver start to deplete, resulting in fat cells releasing fat into the bloodstream which go straight to the liver where they are converted into energy for the brain and body.

Whilst you do not have to link these two principles, a ketogenic lifestyle and intermittent fasting work together to bring the body into ketosis (which scientists are demonstrating leads to a longer and healthier life). The ketotic process releases ketones into the body which release a substance called BPNF that is proven to help memory and energy levels. Studies show that a ketogenic diet can increase your ketone levels four-fold and intermittent fasting gives a 20-fold improvement. Combined, this is a very powerful force.

Going into any further detail is beyond our scope here, but you can find much more information to study online.

The biggest thing for me about the ketogenic lifestyle and intermittent fasting is that it not only helps you to lose weight, but it also stabilises and improves your energy levels like nothing else I have come across as you are no longer subject to sugar spikes and dips.

Whether you believe that a ketogenic lifestyle is the right thing for you or not is going to be down to your personal preference and references. I am not here to tell you what you should or should not do with your health. That, you must work on personally with your own professionals. What I can say is that it works for me. You need to find what works for you as sorting out your energy levels is THE most important thing you can do for your productivity.

Beyond this, the only piece of nutritional advice I will offer is that you must hydrate effectively. Our bodies are made up of at least 60% water, so it stands to reason that water would be a critical element of what we ingest. To be sufficiently hydrated, you should drink at least your body weight of water in ounces every day. That means if you weigh 200lb you should drink 200 ounces of water daily. Also, effective hydration means that you should be constantly sipping your water throughout the day and not just taking large quantities at spaced out intervals. So make sure you always carry a bottle of water with you.

Resistance Training

Aerobic exercise is great, but if you want the full benefit of a powerful dynamic body you should also start to lift weights. The added muscle you build will help to continue to burn your fat stores and you will have an added boost of energy from the structure you create.

I find that a lot of women tend to avoid weight training as they do not want to build bulky muscles in their arms and back. Trust me, it is terribly difficult to build muscles like this and weight training a couple of times a week is not going to turn you into a circus freak!

Sleep

For years, I have actively tried to reduce the amount of sleep I get down to around five hours. I tried alarms sitting at the other side of the room, clocks that would roll off the bedside table and go under the bed so I could not get to them, waking up to empowering music, timer switches on my bedside lamp so it would shine in my eyes, and anything else I could think of. Not only do these things not work, but they also put your marriage in jeopardy! I could do it for a period of time but not consistently, so I decided to take a different approach. Now I let my body do what it wants. I no longer set alarms. I get up when I am ready and I go to bed when I am tired. But the beauty of applying all the principles I have just gone through is that now I am closer to my goal of five hours sleep per day than I ever was before. And all done naturally and not forced. If you treat your body properly, as I have discussed here, then I have personally found that you do not need the eight hours of rest and recovery time we are told we need on average. Why? Because you will not be eating the way average people eat, you will not be exercising the way average people exercise and so you will not need to sleep the way average people sleep.

But, what I would say is don't stress about how much sleep you get. Treat your body properly and learn to listen to when it needs to rest.

And don't be afraid to take a 20 minute power nap in the middle of the day if you start to flag. I have started doing this and the boost I get after a short nap is incredible.

Energy Exercise

Now take a moment and estimate where your energy levels are on average throughout your day on a scale of 1 to 10. If you are like most people reading a book like this you are probably going to overestimate and you might come up with something like a 7 or 8. Now, I want you to take the time over the next three or four days to actually record this hour by hour. Typically, you will find that your average is somewhat lower than your first guess because there are times during the day when you will feel depleted. Please take the time and make the effort to do this as it will spur you on to taking this part of the book as seriously as you should take it. Since I cannot get the answer from you from within the pages of this book, I will assert that you come in with a score 1 to 2 points below where you started, let's say 6.5. This is the real answer.

So why are we doing this? Well, what if you could ACTUALLY improve your physical energy levels by a full two points so you TRULY operate at 8 or 9 or even higher right the way through your day. I am telling you, as long as you apply yourself during the extra time you gain, your productivity is going to go through the roof. This alone can easily double or even triple your levels of productivity because it is not only applied once in a while, as you may do with other techniques, this is available to you in everything you do.

Before we move on, I would like to tell you a brief story about my own experience. Almost four years ago I committed to my own experiment where I decided to exercise every single day of the year – no excuses. I am writing this part of the book on my 1,379th day in a row of exercising. I have not skipped a day for any reason – illness, travel, Christmas Day, New Year, nothing has stopped me. I am now at the point where I am a little OCD about it, but at least it is a good habit! Anyway, as part of this experiment I decided several months ago not to concern myself about my diet too much. I have a pretty good diet, but since I was not focusing on it, some bad habits started to creep in over time. I also found that at my age of 49 (it was very different when I was in my twenties and thirties) my body seems to react a lot faster to bad foods than it does to good foods. The result is that despite not missing a day's exercise in 1,379 days, my weight has been steadily increasing. This tells me that you cannot outrun a bad (or even average) diet. So now, while writing this chapter of the book, I am committing to taking a new consistent approach to an improved diet. This does not mean you should only focus on diet and not worry about exercise – the point is that you need to work on them together, starting with a consistent approach.

If you are not at your peak of health and vitality, you will run out of energy before the day is out. As soon as your energy levels start to drop, your productivity drops with it. It is possible to get up at 5am every morning having gone to bed at 11pm and have boundless energy throughout the day. However, it is not possible to do this unless you look after your body.

Ultimate High Energy Formula

This is my personal formula for spectacular energy:

	Principle	What I do
1)	Consistent aerobic exercise (remember, get here gradually)	45 minutes of aerobic exercise seven days per week
2)	Strength building Resistance training	60 minutes of weight training every other day
3)	Find a diet that energises you from morning until night	Ketogenic diet six days per week
4)	Intermittent fasting	Intermittent fasting from 8pm one day until 12pm the next
5)	Manage your sleep (rest and recovery)	Listen to my body and never set an alarm

But there is one more ingredient that needs to be added to this formula, which is the difference that makes the difference. And that is CONSISTENCY. You cannot dabble in these things and expect to get the results you dream of. You need to apply yourself every day with immutable consistency. You will notice that consistency is the key yet again, as with everything else we have talked about.

If you can apply these five principles consistently, you will start to soar.

And don't tell me you don't have time for this. That is what this book is all about.

Action and Execution

No matter what your energy levels are, unless you put yourself into action, all of that effort is going to be wasted. There are no magic bullets other than consistent execution and action.

The journey of a thousand miles begins with one step.
(Lao Tzu)

Decide – Focus - Action

As I write each section of this book, I think to myself that this is the single most important part of everything I have to say. Indeed, every element is critical to taking control of your life and becoming more productive with your time. But if I have to choose one part that is more critical than the rest, and if you were only to take one distinction away with you when reading this book, make it this one. **Action drives everything**. Without it, all the learning is wasted. Without it, your bad habits will overwhelm your good ones. Without it, you will still be where you are today in ten years' time, and nobody wants that. We all want progress. In fact, Tony Robbins definition of happiness is "progress towards a worthy goal".

There are essentially three steps to getting into action. First, you need to make a decision, then you get you mind focused and then you take the action. Your actions essentially form part of your implementation plan which, in turn, leads to mastery of your subject.

Further, in today's world, speed is of the essence. What you used to do in five years, now you need to do in one or even less. So now is the time to get moving.

Making Shit Happen

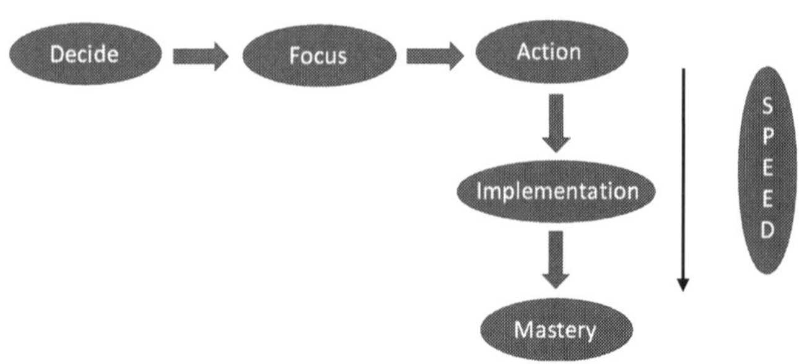

The Progress Formula

Even if you get it wrong, if you make a decision and act now you will find out what doesn't work a lot faster, so you can take a different action in another direction which will inevitably bring you closer to your goals. You need to learn from your actions and keep moving.

I'm not a product of my circumstances, I am a product of my decisions.
(Stephen Covey)

On 4 December 2000, my four business partners and I purchased the business we worked for. I won't name names to protect the guilty(!), but this business had been pretty much run into the ground. It had sales of £240m and losses of £64m in the year we got it. Decision making had been poor for years and the results showed it. As our new Chairman, Mike, took his seat, he knew that things could not go on as they had previously if we were to even survive, let alone thrive. In those first few weeks he had one goal and that was to make things happen. With some of the old executives, who remained with the business for a while, saying "Look you don't understand, you don't have all of the facts. You can't possibly make this decision", Mike just turned around and did it, working from the basis that making no decision had got the business to the point of destruction and by making a decision at least we were moving. If we were wrong, "Great, at least we know now. Let's take action in another direction".

Execution is your single biggest competitive advantage.
(Keith Cunningham)

Clarity is Power

At any stage in what you are doing, there is only ONE thing that should be done NEXT. Everything else is merely noise. So how do you shut out all of the noise and focus on the next thing that will move you forward? The answer to this question, while it may be difficult to find, is actually quite simple. You need to have CLARITY over your outcome.

Whenever you are about to do anything (start your day, make a phone call, go into meeting, anything) ask yourself "What do I want to achieve here?".

You have no idea what you can accomplish when you get clear about what you want. The power you gain from precisely balancing your life according to YOUR rules is staggering. With a clear outcome you can start to formulate a plan of action to get you from where you are today to where you want to be. Without this clarity of objective, you are in danger of aimlessly taking busy actions and getting nowhere. Not only must you be clear about your outcome, you must also be clear about where you are now. Even if you know exactly where you need to be, a map is useless unless you know where you are starting from. If you can spend some time very specifically understanding what juices your life, and you can lay it down in a detailed plan, you are way ahead of the curve.

Risk Profile

You may often be held back from taking action by your fear of what may happen. This is particularly so for people who have established themselves a little. I know that when I was younger, coming into my twenties, and the world was at my feet, whatever I did really didn't matter. I had no responsibilities such as a partner, children or mortgage. If I wanted to travel around the world, I could just get up and go. However, as I moved into my thirties and forties I found myself with all of these things – a wife, two children, two dogs and a big mortgage. Now I had something to lose, and at first this made me think twice before I would take action. Fortunately, I had done some training with some great mentors and managed to step beyond these limits.

One thing that really helps in these situations is to remember past experiences where you took a risk that paid off. I remember back in August 2000, I had been married for almost a year and we wanted to move out of our small two-bed semi into a much more substantial property in the countryside. We found the perfect house. It was a timber framed thatched cottage worth about five times the value of our old house.

So this was a big leap. But this was not the risk. The risk was that I was about to be made redundant from my job. Nothing had been announced, but because of my role in the business I knew what was going on and that there was going to be an announcement very shortly. Now, even back then, no bank in its right mind would give you a mortgage to jump about five rungs up the ladder if you had no job, but we really wanted that house. So during July and August, while I was working on the closure plans for the business, I was also working on buying our dream house. We secured it on Wednesday 30 August 2000 and moved ourselves in over the following weekend. Then, on Monday 4 September 2000 the company that I was working for announced that they were going to sell or close the business.

Now that is a pretty big risk (I am not even sure if it was legal, but don't tell anyone!) but it paid off big time. The story actually goes on because, along with four partners, we bought the business we worked for (which was a complete basket case) and we went on to turn it around during the next three years. We made it hugely profitable and sold it on 4 July 2012 in what can only be described as a fantastic deal.

Now, whenever I have a risky decision to make I always think back to that time in July 2000 when I threw caution to the wind and made two of the most momentous decisions I have ever made – a time when I took action in the face of great uncertainty and got a result that changed my life forever.

If you are waiting until the time is right, the time will NEVER be right. Just do it.
(Unknown)

Actually, to say that I threw caution to the wind really belies the reality of what went on. I am not at all saying that you should take whatever action appeals to you and risk everything you have. I didn't do that. I have actually missed a little bit of the story out. Firstly, I was a qualified Chartered Accountant and very confident in my ability to get a new job, with a pretty handsome redundancy cheque in my pocket. I was also a Finance Executive within the business and so I was very close to what went on in the organisation and I was very confident that the team involved in the management buy-out could right the wrongs of the past executive and make a go of the business we loved. I am not saying that it was not a risk. Of course it was, but it was a well calculated risk. Now, even that calculated risk would have stopped a lot of people from acting, but I took the chance and never looked back.

If you don't risk anything, you risk everything!
(Rob Moore)

Stop Talking Start Doing

This is the title of a great book by Shaa Wasmund. I had been writing my book for about ten years when I went to a bootcamp run by Shaa, a lady who I had never seen before but who came recommended by someone I trusted. The premise of Shaa's book, and indeed the bootcamp, is that in order to get things moving you simply have to get up and do it.

Action is the thing that makes all the difference between a successful person and a failure. But you need to know what action to take and when to take it. One of the great things about the world we live in today is that there are thousands, if not millions, of people out there who have been there and done that and who want to teach you how to do it and get what you want. Learning can be the first part of your action process but it has to be followed up with real nuts and bolts action, where you need to put the rubber to the road and, as Nike says, JUST DO IT. You should always be learning. In fact, one of my key guiding principles is that you should spend 10% of your income on your own personal development. However, you must always remember that your very best learning is done when you are IN ACTION.

You cannot read yourself to six-pack abs! Sometimes you just have to get down and do something.

A good plan violently executed now is better than a perfect plan executed next week.
(George S Patton)

Knowledge is not power. Knowledge is only potential power.
(Tony Robbins)

And don't kid yourself that just because you are doing something, you are in action. Unless your actions are taking you towards your goals or outcomes you are a busy fool.

Vision without action is merely a dream.
Action without vision just passes the time.
Vision with Action can change the world.
(Joel A Barker)

And now is the time to act. Not later.

Often, when we take action we do not get the results we are looking for as fast as we expect to get them, but this does not mean we should stop. In fact, all of your results are going to come from the other side of frustration. You have got to be persistent in the pursuit of your goals, and please make sure you never ever fail because you did not work hard enough. I promise you that this will be the source of deep regret until your dying day. And it makes common sense. You should always work as hard as you possibly can to succeed. After all, if you do a bad job, you spend a lot more time worrying about what might have been and feeling embarrassed about your efforts. If you do a good job, you can pat yourself on the back and move on to the next thing.

Opportunity is missed by most people because it is dressed in overalls and looks like work.
(Thomas A Edison)

The Comfort Problem

I was lying in bed under the sheets early one morning worrying about what I was going to do to make some money and keep my family afloat. I had a lot of things going through my mind and then I thought "Why am I lying here under the covers thinking about this when I could be on the running machine doing exactly the same thing?". And then it struck me – comfort – the biggest killer to progress. And then I thought "What else am I doing because of comfort? If I pushed myself a little harder I could really change things and make a difference.":

- Doing easy administrative stuff in the office rather than getting out there and speaking.
- Not calling people to find speaking opportunities.
- Creating new products rather than getting out there and sharing what I have already put so much time into.

And the only answer to this is in ACTION – getting up, stretching beyond your comfort zone and just doing it.

Importance Versus Urgency

Who is deciding what you are doing on a daily basis? Really think about this question. How much of the stuff you are doing on a regular basis is really IMPORTANT to YOU? How often are you caught up in urgent things that someone else has put on your plate? Where do you spend most of your time? Are you one of those people who is always running in crisis mode and for whom everything is urgent? Or are you constantly in reaction, spending a lot of your time on things that are urgent but at the end of the day are not really that important? Are you always looking for a distraction to get you away from the hustle and bustle of life, mindlessly surfing the web or watching TV, doing things that are neither urgent nor important? Most people sabotage their chances of a healthy well balanced life because they are too caught up in work and other people's agendas to even begin. But the lucky ones – the smart ones – figure out that nothing good will ever happen… until you start the process and stick with it…

The Power of Urgency

Urgency is a state of mind, and it can be a very powerful tool. You need to be able to create a controlled urgency in all you do. Managed correctly, urgency can be a great motivator without being a source of stress. The trick is to make the part of your brain that wants to get things done see the benefits of getting the task done now while still being aware that this is a self-imposed deadline. It is the difference between eustress and distress. Not all stress is negative and the term 'eustress', coined by endocrinologist Hans Selye, refers to the good stress that motivates us and focuses our energy towards the positive feeling of wanting to take control and make things happen now. Distress is the destructive feeling of being out of control. The careful use of deadlines can be the difference between constant achievement of your goals or leaving your dreams on the table.

Urgency is a matter of consequences. If there are no consequences to not doing something, there is every chance you will not do it. The trick here is to create an urgency around what you need to get done by vividly imagining the consequences of not doing it. These consequences can be completely made up as your brain cannot tell the difference between reality and what you vividly imagine.

However, as with everything, there are right ways and wrong ways of creating urgency. It was a standing joke in the office where I used to work that an old boss of ours would always show up about half an hour before the end of the day on a Friday afternoon in order to blow the most minor of issues way out of proportion in an attempt to keep everyone focused on the business over the weekend. Whilst he was trying to create eustress, the timing and nature of how he did it actually only had the effect of alienating everyone and making sure that no-one could relax. In order to create positive eustress within yourself and your organisation, you need to create an empowering vision and a compelling future that will draw people to taking the actions that make things happen.

Motivation and Procrastination

Now we have established that our energy levels are going to give us more bang for our buck than anything else and that we must take action in order to take full advantage of this, why do we still procrastinate?

So, what actually is procrastination and are some people more susceptible to it than others? According to the dictionary procrastination simply means to put something off until later, but we all know that it has much more far reaching implications on our lives than that simple definition portrays. Procrastination can be the driver to low self-esteem and lifelong regret of the things we might have done. To answer the question as to whether some people are more susceptible to procrastination than others, we need to break down the components that lead to this killer of dreams!

Reasons are just excuses in a bow tie.
(Unknown)

In his brilliant book, The Procrastination Equation, Dr Piers Steel, suggests that there are four elements that drive motivation and consequently its twin evil sister, procrastination. The suggestion is that we are motivated by the following formula:

$$\frac{\text{Expectation X Value}}{\text{Time Lag X Impulsiveness}}$$

The principle is that if you have a high expectation of achieving something you are more likely to take action on it. Equally, the greater the value you place on a result, the more motivated you will be to make it happen. By contrast, the longer it takes you to see a result, the less you will be motivated to do something about it now. And further, if you are more susceptible to distraction, this will also slow down your levels of motivation. As we can see from this model, and as common sense would obviously tell us, some people are more likely to procrastinate than others. Whilst all four elements will have different meanings to different people, impulsiveness is probably the one element we can most clearly see as being the driver of different people's behaviour in this regard.

In productivity or time management terms, we would look at this as being all about how easily someone is distracted. In fact, we will focus on distraction management in some detail in the Integration Pillar, as distraction management is essentially the whole essence of what I see as time management.

So, rather than focus any more time on definitions, let's explore some practical ways to eliminate procrastination from our lives, or at least minimise it. After all, there needs to be room for strategic procrastination where we put certain, less important things off while we focus on the big stuff that will move our lives forward. Another way to put this is that we need to prioritise!

I remember seeing Stephen Covey doing his famous 'Big Rock' experiment with a member of his audience. He brought a lady up on stage and asked her to fill a jar with a number of big rocks. When she could fit no more in he asked if the jar was full and, of course, the response was "Yes". So he pulled out a bucket full of much smaller rocks and asked her to put them into the jar, which she did by letting them fall between the gaps in the big rocks. "Now is it full?", asked Stephen. "Yes" was again the response of the lady. You are probably ahead of me here, as Stephen then brought out some gravel, which the lady proceeded to pour within the gaps of the rocks. "How about now?" At this stage, the lady was starting to catch on that there may be more to come. At which point, Stephen brings out a bucket of sand which the lady pours into the jar, filling all the remaining gaps. Looking very pleased with herself, the lady now presents the jar as "completely full". Surely, nothing more can go in, until Stephen finally pulls out a pitcher of water which he pours in until it starts to run over onto the table. Apart from being highly entertaining, the point of the experiment is to show that you can always add more to your knowledge but you can only do this if you lay the foundations (big rocks) first. If you try to do the small stuff first, you will never get to the big and important parts of your life.

Pain and Pleasure

One truism I have found over many years of studying productivity is that it is pain that will get you started but pleasure that keeps you going.

So here are some quick fire procrastination busters that can be used in isolation or combination to get you up and going.

The Power of People

There is nothing better to get you up and moving than the power of community. Whether it be friends, experts, mentors, family or your benevolence towards others, there is something about engaging with others that brings us into action better than anything else. It may simply be that you do not want to lose face in front of a friend or colleague who you have committed to. Or it may be that a family member needs your help and so you move heaven and earth to be there for them. As human beings, we will often do more for others than we would ever do for ourselves so whatever works for you, you should use it.

Also, online communities are a great source of drive for many people. Whatever your problems or dreams, there is a group out there for you to join that is willing to support you. If you are trying to market your services into Facebook Groups, the bigger the group the better. However, if you are looking for inspiration and accountability, I have found that creating your own smaller group serves you much more effectively. It is easy to get your ego tied to trying to create the largest group out there, but one of the best groups I am involved in has only eight members. The reason it works so well is that we all hold each other accountable and we are all looking to help each other and provide unconditional support. No-one is looking to sell anything to each other, we are just there to share and learn.

Starter or Finisher

There are two types of procrastinator. One loves to get new things started but cannot follow through and finish them off and the other is either so busy perfecting current projects or so fearful of opening up more things to do that they cannot get up and get going.

Where do you fit into this spectrum?

Personally, I am more of a completer/finisher. Fortunately for me, my wife is the opposite and loves to start new projects but struggles to finish things off. Whilst this can lead to some frustrations on both sides, it is actually a recipe for really getting things done. Is there anyone that you can team up with to accelerate your own progress by eliminating the starter/finisher procrastination dilemma?

Getting Started

One of the biggest problems for people is getting started and the biggest issue with this is that when you don't just get down and start to work, in your mind you end up building the project into something way bigger than it really is. Something that may only take you ten minutes to do is perceived to be terribly difficult and will take hours to complete. This is often psychological, and the simplest thing can break you free.

Newton's First Law of Motion states that 'an object at rest stays at rest and an object in motion stays in motion unless acted upon by an external force'. Our job in beating procrastination is to recognise negative or positive momentum and then either break it or capitalise upon it.

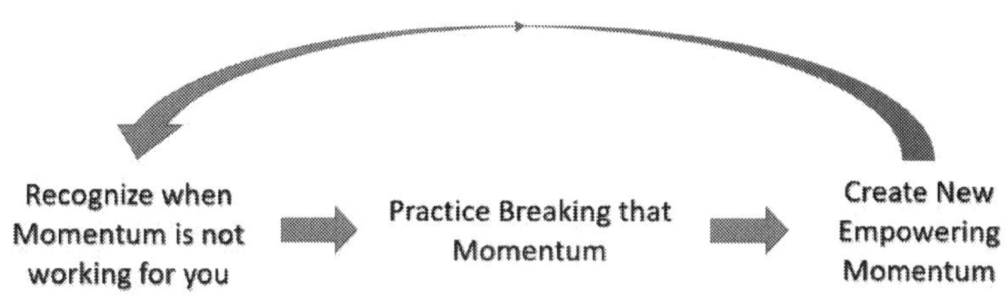

Momentum Cycle

If we are struggling to get started, we need something to help us get moving. It is a little like the analogy of a train at a station – there is an awful lot of effort required to get it moving, but once in motion it tends to keep rolling and then the problem is getting it to stop.

Lots of people identify themselves as procrastinators and feel that this is a genetic trait that they are powerless against. The biggest problem with this is that it becomes a part of a person's identity. You will do anything to maintain integrity with your self-identity, which means that you end up taking actions that promote your procrastination. The truth is that everyone has a tendency to procrastinate. It is just that some people have managed to break its grasp over their lives whereas others wallow in it.

I have personally found that the simplest things, which get the project going, are the most powerful. One very simple example of how a single, supremely easy step can get you moving is to open a document, name it and save it into a folder. That's it! It takes about ten seconds, but I have found it invaluable in so many circumstances.

Why is this so powerful?

Well, the first thing it does is that it tells your subconscious mind that you are ready to get going. The train has started to roll. Not very fast yet, but it is often the first step into motion that is the hardest.

Secondly, you no longer have to think about where to put your next idea. The document is ready for you to type in as much or as little as you like, click Save and you are done. This cuts out part of the thinking process, and while this seems so basic that it cannot be worth doing, just try it and see which projects you can now move on. And once you are in motion, everything becomes much easier.

The Power of One

If you have a project or task that has been on your list for a very long time and you cannot get it moving, try removing yourself from the idea of having to complete the task. For many projects, this can simply be too daunting. The task that takes the longest to complete is the one that never gets started. Instead of trying to get the task completed, set out to take one step towards its completion. This can be something very simple, such as looking up a phone number, logging on to a website or creating a file and saving it into a folder. There is a great power in the one single step; it makes the next step that much easier and tells your brain that you are ready to take action. Everything can get completed one step at a time, but unfortunately many jobs get forgotten because we cannot see through the complexity.

The Power of One also refers to Focus. Everyone likes to think they are great multi-taskers, but this is actually a massive falsehood. You can only ever do one thing at a time that requires focus. If you want to make changes in your life, choose one thing to change and focus all your efforts on that. Mike, a friend and former boss of mine, was a master of this. He would often come into the office in the morning with one outcome in mind. He would set to it and if it was dealt with by 11:30am, he would get in his car and drive home. And believe me, he accomplished far more than other people I have worked for who are running around with crazy timetables and spending most of their time chasing their tails. This is not to say that you cannot do more than one thing in a day. I find it very difficult not to overload my day, but the art of focusing on one task at a time will move you forward faster than anything else I know.

The Power of Timers

Timers are an excellent tool to help you manage your time, and no-one has the excuse of not having a timer as these things are now pretty ubiquitous with any smartphone nowadays. If it is not an integral part of your phone then free apps are available at the click of a button.

A timer is essentially a countdown designed to limit the amount of time you spend on a particular task. We will look into the key timeframes we want to focus on in the next part of this chapter, but essentially what you are trying to do is manipulate your mind into getting into motion. You can use a short amount of time to get yourself moving. Or you can use a larger amount of time to make sure you stay focused on a critical task while ensuring you do not get so caught up in it that either everything else suffers or you get so sick of it that you don't come back to it for a long time.

I also find that using a stopwatch to count up the amount of time I take to do a particular task is very helpful. This is used to best effect when there are tasks you never do because you feel they are going to take too much time out of your day. I will often set the stopwatch running to prove to myself that I only need a couple of minutes to make progress or maybe I only need ten or 15 minutes to complete the whole task. Once I have proved this to myself a couple of times, the next time around I am much more willing to just get down and do it.

The added benefit of the use of timers and stopwatches is that it is great fun. It adds a little bit of interest to an otherwise mundane task and has the further added bonus of getting you laser focused because you only have a small amount of time to work with.

The Power of THREE

Anything you can do within three minutes you ought to just get down and do. This does a couple of things. Firstly, those small nagging items that take up too much of your mental capacity and create stress every time you think about them can be done and out of the way. Secondly, it would take you longer to add the item to your list and come back to it later than it would to simply do it.

One rider to this is that you should guard against these things becoming a distraction throughout your day. You may, therefore, want to set a time aside each day for getting these quick actions done.

Simply doing these small tasks as they appear and planning time to do them is a bit of a contradiction, but both are very valid points. Mastering this trick is part of the art of time management and everyone will approach it slightly differently, so play with it for a few days and see what works best for you.

The Power of FIFTEEN

Fifteen minutes is probably my favourite amount of time! This is great for several reasons. Firstly, it is not a huge amount of time and we can all find a spare 15 minutes in the day. You can easily use a 15 minute window of time to get any big project started. If you have a project that has been on your list for a long time and it seems too large to contemplate, set your timer to 15 minutes and get started. Have no more of a goal than that. The biggest barrier to getting something completed is getting started. Once you are started, you have momentum and you have jumped the most difficult hurdle.

Secondly, once you are in the chair and going, there is every chance that the momentum you have created will turn into half an hour or more and the project gets back on track, or even completed. After all, how many times have you finally got around to doing something that seemed like a mammoth task, only to find that it was nothing like as difficult as you had envisaged.

Beware that you do not go in with the expectation of doing more than 15 minutes every time you start one of these projects. This can defeat the point of giving you the encouragement to simply get started. Every time, go in with the expectation that you are only going to work for 15 minutes so your brain expects this and is not disappointed when you do not go on beyond that timeframe.

Fifteen minutes is also a great chunk of time to cover off all those smaller tasks. The idea here is to isolate into separate lists all those tasks that you estimate will take you 15 minutes or less to complete. This means that whenever you have any spare time or when your energy levels are not quite where you would like them to be, you can go to these lists and knock off a number of things in quick succession. You can also use these lists when you feel the need to tick off lots of things, which we often desire.

The Power of THIRTY

Whilst 15 minutes is great for getting you going, it is not always enough. If I have a big project I find that breaking it down into 30 minute blocks can really make all the difference. It is enough time to make substantial progress, but not so much that you can never squeeze it into your day.

The Power of NINETY

Having just explained the power of short time periods in getting you moving, I am now going to make the opposite argument. The problem with only spending short periods of time working on a project is that you are constantly moving from one thing to the next. Studies have shown that this constant stopping and starting actually affects your productivity in very negative ways.

Let's imagine that you and a friend are going to set off on a 100 mile journey in different cars and with different strategies to get you there. You decide that you are going to pace yourself, you will do 50 miles per hour all the way there and you won't stop for breaks. Your friend on the other hand is a bit of a speed merchant but cannot be out of touch with the outside world for more than ten minutes at a time. He decides that he is going to travel at 100 miles per hour but needs to stop to check emails every ten minutes. The steady 50 miles per hour journey is going to be the most efficient method every time.

I may be slow but I never go backwards.
(Abraham Lincoln)

And so it is with everything else that you do. If you can spend a longer, more focused period working on a project then you will accelerate your progress immeasurably. The problem with this approach is that we often struggle to dedicate several hours in one single stretch to working on the same thing. Trying to find this amount of time in your diary may well mean that you never even get started.

If 30 minutes means that you are changing tack too often and several hours is not sustainable, then where is the sweet spot? The more astute of you will have already answered this question based on the title of this section of the book! Yes, 90 minutes. This is not so much time that you can never fit it into your schedule, but it is substantial enough that you can really get focused and make significant progress. If you have a really big project then 90 minute chunks of time are the way to go. This book is being written in 90 minute blocks of time. Sometimes I might get three or four into a day and other times I might only be able to squeeze one in, but on every day that I do it, I feel myself getting closer and closer to completion.

The Power of Chunking

If you have never run a marathon before, I would advise you not to run 26 miles in order to do it! What you need to do is to run one mile, 26 times. The difference is that you are facing the mammoth task of running 26 miles in small steps that anyone can do. You end up doing the 26 miles, but your focus is never on anything longer than a single mile. You still need to train, of course, but on race day you don't get overwhelmed by the big goal.

Likewise, if you try to list out everything you need to do, which I am actually going to ask you to do later in the book, it is going to get very overwhelming. In order to manage this overwhelm, we can chunk things into more manageable groups of items, which not only reduces down the complexity but also affords you the chance of consolidating several small tasks into a single major project that you can address in a more effective way.

The Dangers of Perfection

Do you identify yourself as a perfectionist? If you do then you need to stop. The concept of perfection is one of the greatest blockages to making progress. Deep down, we all know that perfection does not actually exist. But we often use it as a crutch so we can carry on working in our safe environment rather than getting out there and putting our ideas into action. Perfectionism is really just another form of procrastination.

If you are a perfectionist you need to turn your 'Ready, Aim, Fire' mentality into 'Ready, Fire, Aim'. The problem with aiming before you fire is that the time you are spending aiming is based on your own ideas about what works, but you are getting no external feedback. If you fire first, you are at least going to get some feedback as to whether what you are doing is right or your market even wants it. You then use this feedback to aim before quickly firing again. Every time you fire you are getting real marketplace feedback about what works and what does not work and you are wasting less time in your own head.

You really need to be ready to live by Pareto's 80:20 Rule: 20% of your efforts will get you 80% of your results and you will spend 80% of your time finishing off the last 20%. You should always do your best job, but if you are willing to accept that 80% is good enough you will get five times as many projects moving as someone who tries to perfect everything down to the very last percentage.

If you are not willing to fail, you will not push yourself to the threshold of success.

(Carl Pate)

Confession: The biggest reason for me writing this part of the book is because I need to listen to this advice. I recently had a call with Rick McMunn, my book writing mentor, who was able to see in me what I could not see in myself. Once it was pointed out, it was clear that I had fallen foul of this poisonous trait, and you should always write about something that is close to you.

Tricking Your Brain

Most of the strategies we have talked about in the section of the book on motivation and procrastination are really mind games and psychological tricks to help you move when your natural tendency is not to. But the next three quick tips stand out to me as being simple yet powerful ways to move you to action.

The first I picked up from Tony Robbins when he said that if ever he started to tell himself "I can't" then he had to instantly follow up that statement with "then I MUST". You can make yourself a little OCD with this, but it works: "If I can't, then I MUST."

The second trick is my own take on Tony Robbins' "If I can't, then I MUST!" statement. For me, I started to see things that needed to be done and caught myself thinking "I can't be bothered". Now, if ever I find myself not doing something that needs to be done, I ask myself the quick question "Why?". If the honest answer comes back "Because I can't be bothered" then I have to do it. If the answer is that I am focusing on something else then that is fine, leave it until later but never be caught saying "I can't be bothered!".

Finally, Mel Robbins suggests that if you count down 5-4-3-2-1 when you want to get started on something, this will help to get you going. This method is surprisingly simple, but effective. It seems that counting yourself down into action acts as an effective preparation phase between the stimulus of having the idea and the response of taking action.

Strategic Procrastination

Finally, we need to remember that sometimes it is OK to procrastinate. Strategic procrastination simply means that you procrastinate over the minor things while setting yourself up to move on the majors. Just remember, you cannot do everything, so make sure that what you do counts.

Don't let small things cheat you out of big opportunities.
(Jim Rohn)

Discipline

Discipline is Not a Four Letter Word

Discipline is knowing that when you say something is going to get done, it IS going to get done. But discipline requires structure, especially when you want to apply it across many areas of your life and across multiple activities within those areas. Far from being restrictive, it is hugely freeing. And remember, every good discipline affects everything else. It is like a procession. If you start acting in a disciplined manner in one area of your life, it will start to feed through into everything else and before you know where you are, you will have changed your self-identity to a much more powerful one of being a person of action.

The Power of Disciplined Practice

There is a common myth that practice makes perfect. Actually, practice does not make perfect; **practice makes permanent**. If you continually practice the wrong methods and you are running east chasing a sunset then those incorrect and unhelpful habits will be built into your life. These practices are often the product of the media or other people's desires.

If you pay no attention to the activities you are practicing on a daily basis you are heading down a disastrous path. You need to spend some time setting up a series of routines that you can practice daily and that will move you in the direction of becoming the person you desire to be. Truly successful people can take any aspect of their life and focus on every detail until they become a true master.

There is a commonly quoted rule of thumb that says it takes 10,000 hours of deliberate practice to become an expert in any field. Yes, you can become a master of anything and all that it takes is three hours of hard practice per day, every day, for ten years! But a master is always willing to do what it takes. Every journey starts with a first step. And this could be the first step towards the mastery of your life.

But practice requires constant feedback so you know you are going in the right direction and so you know you are improving. Make sure that whatever you do you have a system to capture everything that is going on around you and I will talk about that later in the book (Daily Life Tracker®).

The 5 Pillars in Action

Commit to maximising your energy levels. Design your own Ultimate Energy Formula.

	Principle	Your Plan
1)	Consistent aerobic exercise (remember, get here gradually)	
2)	Strength building Resistance training	
3)	Find a diet that energises you from morning until night	
4)	Intermittent fasting	
5)	Manage your sleep (rest and recovery)	

Pillar 3 –
BALANCE

Pillar 3 – BALANCE

If your health is good, you are not focusing on your kids... If your family life is good, your business is suffering... If your business is on the up, you may be stressed out of your mind. These are problems the world over. So you need to get focused on what is IMPORTANT to you and work on bringing those things together. Gaining balance in your life is an art, not a science. Only you know when you are out of balance, so it is for you to define what it takes to get back there.

Before we move on, let's establish one thing – absolute balance is not your goal. Balance is a nice idea, but if you are looking for everything in your life to be in balance at the same time then you will be looking forever. Now that is not to say that we should not pursue balance. We absolutely should, but we have to do it in the knowledge that it will always be elusive.

So why bother?

The answer to this question is in the journey. Balance is not a task that you can tick off your list as done. Balance is a dynamic and ever moving goal that you should pursue throughout your life.

Journey trumps destination every time.
(Carl Pate)

Everything is important, but some things are more important than others. Work-life balance is simply not enough today. You need to create whole-life balance across the interrelationship of all the different areas of your life. Now this sounds more overwhelming than it actually is. I have found that everything that exists within my life can be chunked into six categories – Health, Finance, Relationships, Emotions, Personal Development and Life Management. You might change the words and you might distinguish things slightly differently, but in essence this is all there is.

There is a familiar model called the Wheel of Life that gets us to assess how satisfied we are with the different areas of our lives. The more round the Wheel, the smoother our ride through life. Where we have imbalance within the Wheel, this indicates that there are some bumpy moments ahead.

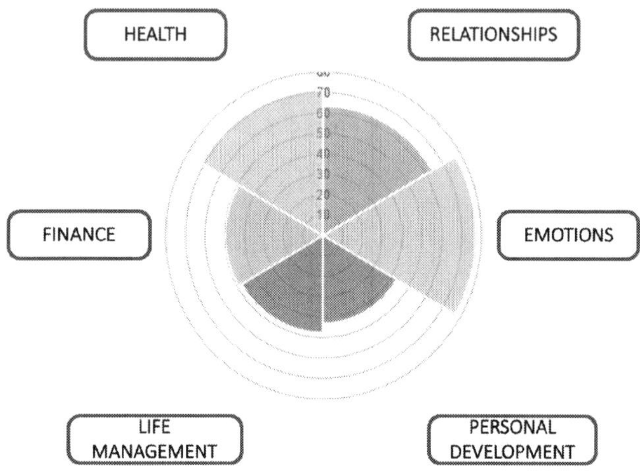

The Wheel of Life

Further, what might feel like balance to you may be exactly the opposite for someone else. And what may feel in balance today may be very different in six months' time. Indeed, balance can feel very different at different stages in our lives. As children, largely unaffected by the outside influences of life, we have little regard for balance and simply play and act in ways that come naturally to us. Unfortunately, this does not last forever and as we reach our twenties and get out into the work place, our balance tends to be focused around a work hard, play hard sense of being. Moving into our thirties and forties brings additional responsibilities of family and mortgages which adds a different dimension to the balance game.

Then as we move into our twilight years, we may reduce our focus on work and start to balance time between grandchildren and travel perhaps. This, of course, oversimplifies the dynamic progression of human life, but I am sure you get the picture. At each of these stages, there are normal and abnormal problems and balance is a constantly moving target that you must flex with otherwise you will live a life of tremendous frustration.

Don't think of balance as a set of scales where you are either one thing or the other. This is why the idea of work-life balance does not quite work. The suggestion is that you are either focusing on your work or you are focusing on your home life and the two compete for your time and energy. But this is not how the real world works. For a start, you cannot go to work and leave you at home, and you cannot be at home and completely switch off from the issues you have at work. In fact, increasingly, we are moving towards a world where we need to embrace the interconnection between our work and everything else within our lives.

Getting in the Zone

We need to think of balance as a zone rather than a target. You can get yourself in the zone by coming up with two or three actions that support you in each of the six categories of your life. These are things that if you do them will make you feel like you are truly taking care of that area, and if you don't will make you feel weakened by it.

Here is a quick exercise:

For best results make sure you do this exercise when you don't feel like you are in the middle of life's chaos. Set 20 minutes or so aside and shut out the rest of the world.

1. Write down the six categories of your life at the top of six sheets of paper (or your version of these categories)

2. For each category complete the following statement with three different answers:

    - I am at my best when…
    - For example, if you are working with your health category you might write "I am at my best when I drink eight glasses of water every day."

In the final Pillar – Tracking – I will introduce you to my unique software, Daily Life Tracker ®, which is equipped to help you record your progress within these principles.

The beauty of this system is that it means that when you get out of balance – which you will – you have a solid track back to your zone where you can constantly return. We cannot expect everything in our lives to be perfectly aligned all the time and neither do we want it to be. Progress requires you to focus very keenly on what you are working on and that means you must come out of balance. The secret that the masters know, but few others do, is to first know when you are going too far off track. Then, more crucially, knowing exactly where that central core is AND then being able to get back to it no matter what is going on in your life. Balance is a ZONE, not a lifestyle or a specific point.

How would it feel if you were able to quickly snap yourself back into your most powerful state no matter what your challenges? If you know where balance is for you because you have created a plan when you were in a rational mood, then it is easy to get back on track. Trying to do this when everything is out of control is a much more challenging prospect.

Bruce Lee came up with the idea that you should 'be like water' and this is how you should think of balance. Imagine an ocean with all the different elements of your life resting on the waves. Your goal is to have a nice calm ocean where everything rests in a steady state, but this is unrealistic. Sometimes the ocean appears calm but there is always movement, and movement is just a sign of life. Sometimes the ocean is dramatically turbulent and it seems like it will never steady. No matter how much you work on one area, the turbulence continues. This is when we feel most out of balance, when every area of our life is in apparent chaos. We will also find that if one area of our life is turbulent, it affects all the others. Maybe not to quite the same extent but, all the same, it rocks the boat.

The 'be like water' analogy goes further. Imagine you are sitting next to a perfectly still lake and you toss in a rock. How does the water react? The answer is that the water reacts in absolute proportion to the size of the rock you threw in. If you threw in a tiny rock, you will see small waves emit from the centre. If you threw in an enormous rock, water will go everywhere and the turbulence will be felt much more widely and for a much longer period of time. This is how you need to treat issues that come into your life; in a measured way that is proportionate to the size of the problem you are facing. Don't overreact and don't underreact – react in a balanced manner.

No matter how busy you are or how out of control your life feels today, there are certain key principles that when understood and put into action will give you the feeling of calm, controlled confidence. Whatever is going on around you, you can get to that powerful, centred core of who you really are… where you are in control. This simply takes a little up-front analysis of what works for you and it will soon put you back in the driving seat of your life where you feel in control of your own destiny like never before. If you are ready to take action and end the chaos around you once and for all, you really can change your entire life. Starting today.

Taking control of your life is all about setting a plan. If you have already thought through a situation before a crisis hits you, then you are much better prepared to cope. You just need to set up plans to support every area of your life. So when something goes out of control – and it will because that is life – you will know exactly what to do to take control again. You don't have to panic and think up solutions on your feet. You can just get on and do it.

What is Balance for You?

What you need are a few simple routines, or habits, in each of the areas of your life you wish to master. These are the things that make you strong and make you feel in control, such as a daily run to help get your health back on course. When you feel yourself getting out of balance, check in with what you have been doing or not doing in the other areas of your life and make some adjustments to put it right. But this is where the art comes in. Only you know when you are going out of balance. Only you know what it takes to get back there. In actual fact, even you may not really know the answers to these questions. So test it! If what you do does not work, try something else, and if something does work, do more of it.

Whilst you should not stress out about always being perfectly balanced, you should always be aiming to get a balance in your life without being too extreme in any direction. The key is to get the balance between FLEXIBILITY and SELF DISCIPLINE. When you have this, you are in your PRIME STATE. Flexibility is crucial to a happy life. And discipline means when you say you are going to get something done you and everyone around you knows it is going to get done. We all know someone who is overdisciplined and far too rigid in everything they do. It is black or white and there is no in-between. But these people are generally highly stressed and there are huge health risks associated with this. Learning to let go is a real challenge, but when you do it, it is like you switched channels on the TV and a whole new world opens up. Here, I speak with a lot of experience, as I am one of those people!

Then there is the other extreme of person – those who are supremely flexible. You know the type, they can never remain focused on one thing for more than five minutes. They never take anything very seriously. To these people, discipline is a four letter word! It is their life and they will live it their way. They find no issues with being late wherever they go. "I am an adult, I will decide what I do and when I do it." Of course, this is often to the detriment of those around them and more importantly they never get anything done. And a life without some sort of achievement and contribution to the world around you is pretty hollow. The goal is to get a balance between flexibility and discipline.

Balance is a feeling not a thing. No matter what is going on in your world, it can feel like you are out of balance. Even if you are handling all the different categories of your life perfectly well, you can still feel out of balance if your mind is not on the task at hand. It is very easy when you are at work to be worrying about something that you should have done at home, and when you are playing with the children you might have your mind on a work project. The problem with this affliction is that you never feel at ease and as a result it feels like your life is out of balance. The problem here is not that you are out of balance, but that your attention is on something else.

Wherever you are, be there.
(Jim Rohn)

The trick here is quality not quantity. If you make something too big in your head, you often end up doing nothing at all. Just because you don't have three hours to spend with the kids should not prevent you from spending 20 quality minutes with them. Getting balance back into your life doesn't have to take up lots of your time.

You should not be 'butterflying' from one thing to the next because you cannot settle on what to do. This is about planning quality and focused time in each of the categories of your life.

The other thing that makes you feel out of balance is when you forget to be grateful for what you have. Having an 'attitude of gratitude' is a great answer to all sorts of problems and life balance is one of them. If ever you feel out of balance, take six pieces of blank paper and head each page with one of your life categories, as we have already talked about. Then set a timer for 15 minutes and write down everything you are grateful for in each of these areas of your life. Don't stop writing until your 15 minutes are up and then at the end of this exercise see if your life feels a little more balanced. If one or two of the pages look a little blank then this is a clue as to what you need to be working on. If they all look pretty full then maybe the problem is one of perception rather than reality.

Workstyle Balance

How does your work life look? I recently went to a networking event where the speaker talked about the evils of modern technology and how in today's world of smartphones and wifi we are never able to switch off. He talked about taking vacations where you never used or even took your technology with you. In the speaker's eyes, this would allow you to recharge your batteries and give you a much needed balance to your life. Now, you will recognise from the pages of this book that I am all about balance, but it has to be real world balance and there are a couple of points about this principle that we should explore.

Firstly, to operate like this is not the real world and particularly not the world in which the next generation of business people and entrepreneurs are growing up and creating. If we believe that our children are going to take two weeks where they never switch on their smartphones then we are very deluded. It is almost like telling them to stop breathing for two weeks. And this is only going to get more prevalent as technology advances faster and faster. So, we need to start to look at the world in a new way.

This brings me to my second point. There is currently an increasing movement of people creating a mobile workstyle where they can work from anywhere in the world because of the technology that they have available. Technology is never the enemy. The enemy is the way we use this technology. If you are going to sit working all day every day and never switch down then this is a problem that will lead to enormous amounts of stress. However, if you can design your workstyle such that it actually becomes your lifestyle then you are starting to advance to a new level. By using your technology effectively, you can be sitting on a beach operating your business from a smartphone or tablet for 52 weeks of the year. Now you are starting to create lifestyle balance throughout the whole year, rather than just for an isolated two or four week period. To some, it may look like you never switch off, but in reality it is quite the opposite. Now there are some jobs, of course, where you cannot do this, but increasingly in our service-based economy there are more and more opportunities to create a workstyle and lifestyle that seamlessly gel together.

Is this really balance?

Changing Environment

One of the most exciting and beautiful things about life is that it is dynamic and always moving, so you can never just rest and say that you are done. You are always moving from one stage to the next – your body's reaction to your lifestyle will change with age, raising a family is a constantly changing environment as your children or relationships move from one stage to the next and your career and financial needs keep moving. There is a constant disruption and need to realign what you are doing. The results you got from your actions in your twenties are different to the results you will get in your forties – this applies as much to your body as it does to your relationships and your finances.

There are also seasons to life. Jim Rohn actually wrote a whole book on this subject called The Seasons of Life. Sometimes your life will feel like you are in a deep winter as difficulties pile one on top of the other. But then winter is always followed by the promise of spring where you start to see new opportunities for growth. Summer is sure to follow as those opportunities turn into reality, which then turns into the reaping of your rewards in the autumn. Some seasons are short and we may hardly notice them and others may be long and deep, but we will always come out of them. It is a great thought to believe that no matter how dark your days seem to be, you will always find a way through. But you must also beware the long and prosperous autumn, as this will undoubtedly be followed by winter. We all go through this and recognising it does not make you a pessimist, just a realist. There is nothing wrong with winter. If you are prepared for it, you can build a snowman and take advantage of the situation with the knowledge of a brighter future to come. There is a great opportunity in recognising what stage of life you are at because you can mould your actions and life accordingly. The point here is that while sometimes things might look like they are starting to go wrong or out of control, there is always hope and belief that you will come through it. You can set plans for a new stage of your life, regain control and get even better, more fulfilling results than ever before. But this is about managing and taking control of your life. And, again, this is an art rather than a science.

So far, I have focused the message of balance on the categorisation of life across its many aspects. But you also need to balance your life across time periods. This is best demonstrated in a diagram:

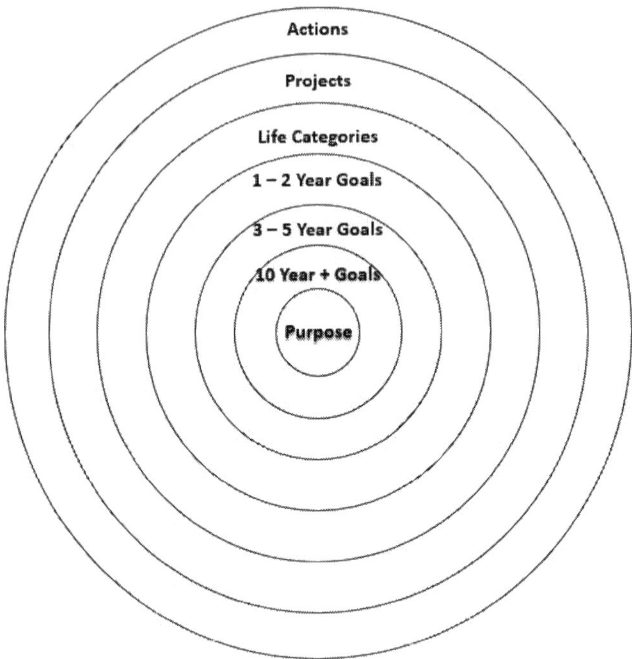

Balance your outlook over time

The central core of this diagram focuses on your life purpose and then we work our way back through ten year goals, three to five year goals, one to two year goals and then into our six life categories. From there, we have projects that fit into each of the life categories and then actions within those projects. The idea is to design your life in such a way that your daily actions flow through to your life purpose. The balance aspect of this relates to where you focus your time throughout this chart. If you are purely action focused, your life will centre around your immediate needs and this is where you will find yourself too busy to think. If you focus purely on purpose, you are just a dreamer.

Balance in Everything

While the focus of this chapter is on how we balance all the different areas of life, here are a few other things you might want to apply the principle of balance across. This is not a complete list, of course, but it is designed to get you thinking about how rigid your views might be about certain things and whether you ought to look to even things out a little:

- Risk versus Reward
- Work versus Play
- Enthusiasm versus Control
- Do versus Learn
- Feedback versus Criticism
- Patience versus Impatience
- Self versus Family versus Others
- Success versus Failure
- Past versus Present versus Future
- Major projects versus Minor projects

I hope this chapter demonstrates that it is not all about running at 100 miles per hour chasing your goals; you need to get a good balance between all the areas of your life and sometimes you just need to slow down and smell the roses.

Don't just do something. Stand there!
(Rochelle Myer)

The 5 Pillars in Action

Create your Zone: Identify the different categories of your life that you would like to gain balance over.

Design two actions in each category that will support that part of your life by completing the statement 'I am at my best when…'

Sample Zone	Your Zone
HEALTH	
Aerobic exercise for 45 minutes per day five days per week	
Drink 200 ounces of water every day	
FINANCE	
Spend one hour working on a new business project four days per week	
Make ten sales calls five days per week	
RELATIONSHIPS	
Date night with partner one day per week	
Spend 60 minutes with the kids five days per week	
EMOTIONS	
Meditate for ten minutes per day five days per week	
Write down five things you are grateful for five days per week	

Pillar 3 – BALANCE

PERSONAL DEVELOPMENT	
Read ten pages of inspiring material five days per week	
Write a journal entry five days per week	
LIFE MANAGEMENT	
Spend one hour planning the other 23 hours every day	
Clear your desk every night before bed	

Pillar 4 –

INTEGRATION

Pillar 4 – INTEGRATION

So this is where we put it all into action. Having built the foundations where we have mastered our habits, worked on ourselves and understanding of how we move everything forward in a balanced and integrated manner, we are now ready to assimilate some new high productivity strategies into our lives. In this Pillar, we will look at the nuts and bolts techniques and strategies that will multiply your personal productivity two-fold, five-fold or even ten-fold or more.

Some of these strategies are not going to be new, but what is new is that you now have a firm foundation on which to build them so, unlike before, you will be able to introduce any new concepts and keep them with you long term.

Whatever you are doing, you need to go in with a plan. You need to be flexible enough to change your approach as your circumstances change – which may be frequently – but you need to go in with a plan. This applies to both your whole day and to individual tasks you have to do throughout the day. There is a reason that the saying "If you fail to plan, you plan to fail" is such a cliché. Planning can help reduce stress and minimise distractions because when you have the clarity of a plan, you always have your next move in hand.

Give me 8 hours to chop down a tree and I will spend the first 6 sharpening the axe.
(Abraham Lincoln)

Distraction Management

Your inability to get things done is not usually a question of time management. It is a question of DISTRACTION MANAGEMENT.

It is useful to have a working definition of what we mean by distraction because distractions often come disguised as noble, interesting or exciting opportunities. When we are thinking about distractions in respect to personal productivity, we mean anything that takes you off task. A phone call while you are in the middle of a meeting is an obvious distraction, but so is one of your kids who is crying because they have hurt themselves. Also, by reason of this definition, the task you are working on now may well become a distraction in the future. If you are playing with the kids and an important business call lights up your phone, this is a distraction from the important task of playing with your kids.

Monitor what you do very carefully during the day. At the end of the day, look at your productivity. When you lost focus what caused it? Almost always, it will be some sort of distraction. This could be the TV, the internet, the phone or the annoying email bleep when a message comes in. Now I am not saying that you should not deal with the interruption, or indeed never succumb to any other type of distraction, but you must recognise it for what it is so you can deal with it and minimise these occurrences.

It is estimated that around 25% of your time is taken up recovering from distractions, which is a staggering waste of time. Studies also show that once you have been distracted it takes you at least 11 minutes to regain your focus to the point that it was at before the distraction took place. If this is the case, that four minute phone call cost you 15 minutes of focused time. Four calls that you pick up or email bleeps that you respond to and you lose one hour of your day. The telephone (especially the mobile phone) and email are the worst culprits for this. When I am in a meeting, I never answer the phone. Often, this can make my colleagues very uncomfortable. “Aren’t you going to answer that?”, “No, you are more important at the moment” I will say. You would think this would make them feel good but you can see the discomfort in their face as they say “But how do you know that I am more important. Are you sure you don’t want to answer it?”. That is what voicemail is for! Let it do its job and then return the call once you have completed your current task – or better still at a specific time allocated to replying to calls.

You would be surprised how much of your day is affected by distraction. One very powerful exercise is to create a distraction log where you record the time and nature of every distraction that occurs throughout your day. You should also include what you do when the distraction happens – whether you succumb or resist – how much time it took from you and how you might avoid this happening in the future. The mere fact that you are recording these distractions will help you as you will become much more conscious of what you are doing. Ironically, this may mean that the distraction log is not as reflective as it might be of a real day in your life when distractions occur without you even noticing. A truer reflection would require a secret camera crew following you around and recording the distractions for you, but now I think we are going a little bit too far! The ultimate goal is to stop the distractions, so this is actually a good thing. When you review this log at the end of the day you must work on implementing solutions to avoid these distractions in the future. This is all part of your incremental growth and will pay huge dividends down the line.

Parkinson's Law

Parkinson's Law is the adage that 'work expands so as to fill the time available for its completion'. Whatever time you have, you will use. The reasons for this are two-fold. Firstly, you may try to work on 'perfecting' something that does not need to be improved upon. And secondly, when you have more time on your hands you are more vulnerable to distractions.

The devil will make work for idle hands to do.
(Unknown)

With less time available, you are likely to be more focused and less distracted. With more time available, you are likely to be less focused and more distracted.

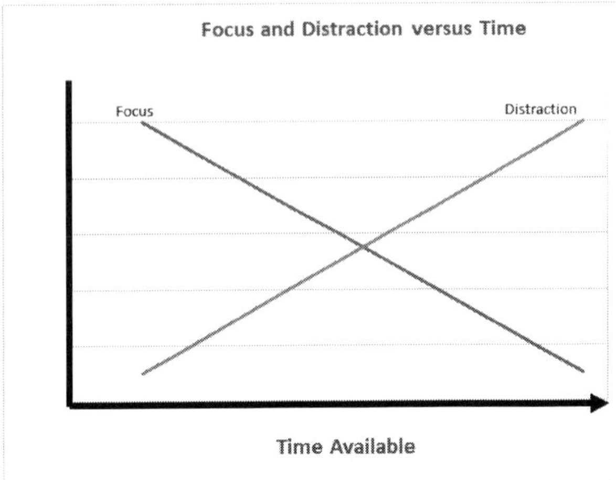

Focus versus Distraction

This is a big issue for people who always seem to be late for whatever they are doing. When running a few minutes ahead of time, they develop a strange sort of easiness about them that slows their flow and heightens their likelihood of getting distracted.

The real trick is to create an urgency in your own mind even when there is no real need for it.

So how do we set ourselves up to minimise these distractions?

Start Your Day The Night Before

For most people their day starts when the alarm goes off in the morning. If you are smart, however, you should start your day the night before. What does this look like?

Get Your Body Ready

First and foremost, this requires you to think about how you are treating your body and whether you are setting yourself up for a bright and energetic leap out of bed or whether there is every likelihood that you will pull the sheets over and snooze the alarm four or five times before you reluctantly drag yourself to the bathroom. What you eat or drink, how much you eat or drink and when you do it is critical to the quality of your sleep and how you will feel in the morning.

Get Your Mind Ready

This, of course, also involves planning what you are going to do the next day. If you don't know what you want to do tomorrow morning, you won't get excited enough to throw the covers off and get up. So make sure you set your plans, and make sure that they are engaging.

Many studies have proven that your brain reorganises your thoughts and works on your ideas while you sleep. If you plan what you want to do in the morning at the end of the previous day your brain will start working on it while you sleep, and you will be off to a running start as soon as you get up.

Furthermore, if you have planned your day the night before you can get started as soon as you get up and you can avoid the drag of early morning thinking.

Get Your Environment Ready

Next, think about the things you know you are going to need to do in the morning and that could easily be prepared for the night before. A good example of this might be getting your clothes ready or putting the kids' school bags in the car. These are not things that are going to revolutionise your life but if you believe in the 'aggregation of marginal gains' which I discussed at the beginning of the book, then all these things are built to cumulate into something much greater than the individual parts.

You should also use this time to get your desk clear (if you have a desk) so that everything is fresh and tidy for the start of a new day. A cluttered desk creates a cluttered mind and many distractions to stop you moving forward most effectively.

Early Morning Procedure

No matter what goes on during the day, you always need to start it. This is the only part of your day that you might be able to predict. So make sure you use this time properly. Start off by exercising or with 90 minutes of focus on your grandest outcome. Don't start by checking Facebook and never look at your emails first thing in the morning before getting going. Firstly, you don't want someone else to be creating your day for you. And secondly, it distracts you from doing what you need to do. No-one will be expecting a response that early in the morning and if an email attracts your attention, you will be thinking about it when you should be relaxing or exercising, or it will take the focus from the big project that you might be working on!

Planning is Real Work

There are essentially three types of work – planned work, unplanned work and planning work. Most people recognise the planned work as being the work that you find on your to-do lists, but they generally see this as being the only real type of work that has any validity in taking up their working day.

Generally, the unplanned work is seen as an interruption that really should not be getting in the way of you doing your real (planned) work. However, this type of work has just as much of a place in your working day as the planned work does. In the dynamic world in which we live, there is always something new coming at us: conversations, meetings, phone calls, emails and any number of other sources. As this work comes to you, you need to quickly assess it. Can it be delegated to someone else, does it need to go into your lists (see below) or can it be done within three minutes, in which case you should just go ahead and do it?

The third type of work is where you do your planning. This is very much 'thinking' work and is where you reflect upon and review everything you have to do and decide how it fits into your life plan. Where is your time best spent today? What outcomes do you want to achieve this week? Where do you see your life heading in the next 12 months? If you are anything like me, this can be the source of much guilt. When I first started out, this didn't feel like work at all and I would generally do all of my planning in my own time because I felt so guilty about doing what I saw as non-value added work while on the clock. I have now come to understand that this is probably the most critical type of work. A couple of hours spent thinking and planning your time will make you so much more efficient and you will save far more time in the long run as a result of setting this time aside.

I now spend about one hour every day planning how I am going to use the other 23 hours. The language here is critical. If I suggest that you spend one hour a day planning, that sounds like another task is being added to your workload and you are unlikely to do it. If I suggest you spend one hour planning the other 23 then this places the focus on what you could get done in those 23 hours. This is more likely to result in you doing it. This does not have to be 60 straight minutes and I tend to spend about 20 minutes, three times a day, planning the next few hours.

Plan Like Fedex

Fedex are a worldwide distribution company that prides itself on delivering your packages by the very next day. To do this, it needs an extremely sophisticated planning system that involves a hub and spoke structure. No matter what the destination, everything is routed through a central hub.

This is not going to be a Fedex case study or even an in-depth look at how Fedex might plan their routes, but this is simply the mindset I like to put myself in when I start my weekly or daily planning.

The first thing I consider is the hub and spoke nature of a planning system.

Central Planning System

Pillar 4 – INTEGRATION

While you have multiple areas of your life to consider and many subsections below, everything needs to be managed from one central location. I personally use my Daily Life Tracker ® software to manage all of this, but whatever system you use it should all be done from one location. This makes everything much easier to manage and means that you always know where to go in any situation.

Now, on to the planning itself. If you were running Fedex would you create a plan for the driver and stick to it? Of course, you would.

Can you imagine if an irate customer calls one of the drivers on their mobile phone when he is about to make a delivery in Edinburgh and tells him that it is imperative that he deliver their package to London first. Then another customer calls and gets the driver to deliver the next package to East Anglia. Of course, in a Fedex-type scenario this is ridiculous and no-one would ever allow this to happen otherwise they would be out of business in a very short time. But this is the way most people operate their own lives. They let the person who shouts loudest determine what they do next and as new emails come in this is what determines their next actions. In your own life you need to act in a Fedex style, so once you have a plan you stick to it. Now, of course, in the real world there are constant updates to your plans and tasks. Some things will drop off and some will be added on, so you need to be flexible and move dynamically with all new information. But at every point in the process, you need to be building a new plan that now caters for the new situation. This can feel a little contradictory at first, but this is the nature of a dynamic plan. Know exactly where you are going now, but be ready to reshape as things change.

So, tell me, if you were running Fedex, would you take an hour out of your day to plan your drivers' routes?

Frequency of Plans

Now we have established that planning is critical to your success, how often should you plan?

The answer to this question varies, of course, according to your timeframes.

Medium to Long Term Goals

When considering your one, three, five or ten year goals and even your life purpose, this does not really need to be addressed any more than once per year. The Goals section later in this Pillar looks at this process in more detail and you can also visit our online resources where we have created a real time Goal Setting Workshop for you to go through.

Short Term Goals

These can again be picked up as part of your annual Goal Setting Workshop but you should also revisit them on a more frequent basis to check their continuing relevance. For instance, your one year goals should be broken down into quarterly sub-goals and then the next quarter should be broken down into three monthly plans. These do not have to be detailed in their nature but more like milestones you can use to make sure you are on track.

Weekly Outcome Plans

This is where we start to get into the proper planning. Most of your planning activity should be based around your weekly and daily plans.

For the most part, your weekly plans should be based on outcomes or results. What are the key things you want to achieve this week? You do not necessarily need all the detailed steps to be in place during this part of the process, just the overall outcome, such as write the next chapter of your book or create a two hour online course.

Remember to be realistic with your weekly plans. It is better to have three weekly outcomes that you hit than 20 that are all missed because you could not get focused and your time was spread too thinly.

Daily Action Plans

Now, your daily plans should be a little more granular and more action oriented. The actions you plan for your day should, of course, reflect the outcomes you have set for the week. This is where you actually start to make things happen.

However, even your daily planning needs to start with an outcome focus. I like to think of this as **3-1-1 Planning**.

First write down the **THREE OUTCOMES** you must achieve and that if you do achieve them would mean you go to bed happy with your accomplishments.

Next, look at those three outcomes and decide which is **THE ONE OUTCOME** you absolutely definitely must do before the end of the day, even at the expense of the other two and anything else. Ask yourself "What if I got to the end of the day and I had only accomplished this ONE thing. How would I feel?".

Then you can move from outcome to detailed actions. Brainstorm the actions you need to take to achieve your outcome and build them into your lists. Lists get their own detailed section in the following pages.

The final 1 in the 3-1-1 planning system refers to your very **NEXT**

ACTION. No matter what you are doing, make sure you know what you want to be doing next. I will talk about this in some more detail later, but the best way to avoid distractions after you have finished a particular task is to move straight onto the next one. The only way you can do this is if it is pre-planned.

3 – Plan three **outcomes** for the day
1 – Decide on the single most important **outcome** of all
1 – Always know your very next **action**

The Power of Lists

Before I get into this section, I need to put something to bed. I have recently heard a lot of discussion about whether you should or should not use to-do lists. Let's get it straight, the answer to this question is an emphatic YES. Even some very prominent players in this space are advocating getting rid of your to-do lists, but they are wrong. Actually, whenever you listen to what these people really have to say, they still come back to the use of lists. What they are actually saying is that you should not have random useless lists. And if a senior person in an organisation tells you that they don't use to-do lists, I can guarantee that there is someone in the background who is running one on their behalf.

A little while ago, I saw a Facebook post from a guy who was trying to get people to stop using to-do lists. In the article, he raised the question: Do you think that Bill Gates, Richard Branson or Steve Jobs use to-do lists? Even though his article went on to explain why they did not use to-do lists, the part that caught my eye was the response he got from none other than Richard Branson himself. He dismissed the blogger's assertion that Richard Branson did not use to-do lists as nonsense. In fact, he went on the make the case that everything he had built was because he DID use to-do lists. He said he always carries a notepad with him to make notes and lists wherever he goes. Branson's one corollary of this was that they had to be **TO-DO** lists that get done and not just a list of random thoughts that sit there and end up frustrating you at the end of the day.

So yes, I agree, don't have crap to-do lists, have good, effective ones. A proper, well structured list will enable you to be productive no matter how much time, energy or drive you have. This is going to be what we examine in this part of the book.

The big lesson for me is that you need to write everything down.

The first thing you need to do is get everything out of your head and into your system (which we are about to discuss), which will free your brain to do what your brain is supposed to do; be creative. Your brain is not designed to store all the stuff you have to do today; life is far too complex. But once you get everything out of your head and into your system, this can get a little scary. You see, for most people their lives and what they do next is determined by their inbox and the world around them. But if you can get everything out of your head and into your system then **YOU** get to decide what you do next because basically you have everything under control. This can look a little overwhelming at first, but just because you do not put something into your list does not mean it does not have to be done. What it does mean is that it is stored somewhere in your brain and will not surface at an appropriate time. Having a powerful and effective list not only allows you to make a best judgement on what to do next but it also helps you to get comfortable with what you are not doing.

So, what makes a good list?

Life is complicated and our lists need to reflect this. They need to be sophisticated enough to manage the complex, multifaceted nature of our lives, but at the same time they need to be simple and effective, adding clarity to an otherwise chaotic environment. There is a crossover here with the Planning part of this Pillar as a good plan is going to end up being contained within your list structure. One of the biggest gains you get from planning your lists is that most of your thinking is done up front. When you get to the end of one task, you can move straight on to the next one and it cuts down the friction of thinking between tasks. Do your planning once, create your structure and then tweak it throughout the day.

I spend about 20 minutes of my planning time getting intimate and engrossed in my various lists. This may sound a little odd at first, but this approach yields huge advantages. Your planned work becomes much more efficient and your unplanned work is allocated much more effectively. But what do I mean by saying that you need to become intimate with your lists? This is not some perverted control freakish nature coming out, although it may appear that way. In order to understand this, we need to understand the nature of the lists we are talking about. I propose that you need two lists to run your life, or three if you include your calendar as a list.

1) Master List

I consider this to be a 3-D list where you are able to look at the same information from three different dimensions. Firstly, there is the Master List itself, which is a categorised list of everything you need to do. Secondly, you need to view your list by context so you only look at relevant tasks in any situation. Thirdly, you need to be able to allocate a timing to these tasks so you have a plan for your day or week.

So let's look at each in turn.

Pillar 4 – INTEGRATION

The Master List is possibly the most important list of all in terms of relieving the stress or sense of overwhelm that most of us feel, but it is the list that 99% of people will resist doing properly. To work properly, this list needs to be a complete inventory of EVERYTHING you have to do in your life, not just your work but your personal life too. If this list is complete, it will relieve your stress levels more than anything else you could do. This is because much of the worry about the stuff you need to get done comes from the fact that it is kept in your head where you will repeat the same things over and over again, convincing yourself that you have far more to do than is, in fact, the case. When you get everything down into a master list, and I mean everything, you will feel a huge sense of relief.

This list should not just be random. Start by categorising your life into its key components. This might sound rather daunting but, as mentioned previously in the book, I have found that I can pretty much cover everything I need to do, or look after in my life, into the six categories of Health, Relationships, Emotions, Finance, Personal Development and Life Management. There isn't anything that does not fit these categories for me – yours may be slightly different but I venture that they will not be too far removed.

You will then need to subcategorise these areas of life focus and this is where it starts to get a little more personal, but once you have chunked your life into these six categories then the next level becomes much easier. Depending on how complex you want your structures to be, there could be multiple layers here. For example, a subcategory to Finance might be the company where you work (since this is where you make your money) and a subcategory to that might be that you are responsible for customer relations. See example structure below.

Physical Mastery

- Action
- Action

Emotional Mastery

- Action
- Action

Finance

- XYZ Company LLC
    - Customer Relations
        - Action
        - Action
    - Personnel Matters
        - Action
        - Action
- Manage investments
    - Action
    - Action

Contexts

The next thing you should consider is the context in which you are working. This is simply another way to view the items within your Master List. This essentially refers to your location or environment and it enables you to only see the items on your list that you can do in the situation you are currently in. It is probably best explained by example. If you are at home, you only really want to see the things on your list that you can do at home. If you are in the office, you only really want to be looking at things you can do when you are in the office. And if you are sitting waiting for your partner to get ready for a night out, it might be useful to have a list of all the phone calls you can make while you are waiting. The trick here is to only be reviewing the stuff you are able to do at that time. If you are looking at anything else, you are starting to lose efficiency.

Sample contexts include:

- Home
- Office
- Calls
- Agendas
- Errands
- Anywhere
- Car
- Email
- Mobile
- Online
- Computer
- Waiting for
- Future

These are essentially your working to-do lists.

Timing

The next way you might want to look at your lists is by timing. What do I need to do:

- Today
- Tomorrow

- This Week
- Next Week
- Soon
- Later
- Any Time

I would tend to group Today and Tomorrow together. At the start of the day, there will generally be nothing in my Tomorrow list but as the day moves on items that are not going to get completed today get rolled over and new items that come in but cannot be done today get put onto the Tomorrow list for later consideration. Towards the end of the day, when I start planning the following day, I will review the Tomorrow list and see whether those items move forward to Today or back to This Week. I also group together This Week and Next Week and this works in exactly the same way as described for Today and Tomorrow.

There are lots of tools out there that can help you with this, but I use and highly recommend our own Daily Life Tracker ® as this elegantly enables all of this with a single point of input for your actions.

Weekly Outcome List

- This Week
- Next Week

The first of your timed lists should be the list of things you want to get done this week. This list is best managed as an outcome focused list.

Whatever you want to call it, knowing exactly where you are aiming and your goals, outcomes or targets is a critical element of the planning process. Without knowing your ultimate outcome, you cannot possibly hope to get there. The process here is to come up with two or three major outcomes for the week in each of the critical areas of your life.

Having a clear outcome to work towards during the week focuses your mind on what is important to you and gives you the opportunity to make real progress towards your goals. Clarity is power and lack of clarity leaves you stumbling in the dark.

Daily Action List

- Today
- Tomorrow

This is where the rubber hits the road. What are you going to do today? This list needs to be very ACTION focused. An action is something you can actually do. For example, Call Dave (07777-777777) about landscaping project. Note here that I have included a telephone number so I can make the call. Without this, the next action would be to actually find the phone number. The actions on this list should be driving towards the achievement of your weekly outcomes. However, other things will come up that need to go onto the list, so you need to find a place for these too.

One other great tip here is to create an ORDER to your daily action list. That means, what will you do first, second, third and so on. This does not mean what is most important, it is simply the order in which you are going to do things. In my experience, I have found that most time is wasted between actions. When I am focused on getting something done, I can get it done. However, when I have finished, unless I know exactly what I am going to do next, I am open to all sorts of distractions that will waste my time. By creating an order to the actions, you can eliminate some of this problem.

Now, having said all of this, you need to remember that we are living in a dynamic, ever changing world and so you need to be prepared to be flexible if your circumstances change during the course of the day, which they will. If things have changed, you may need to re-order your list, but if not, you can just move straight on to the next task.

Beware of projects or outcomes on your lists. You cannot DO a project as a project is made up of a series of actions. In order to make progress on a project or outcome, you need to break it down into its next actions. If there is something that has been on your list for a very long time, chances are you have not broken it down into clearly defined actions that you can actually do.

2) Daily Habits and Rituals

The next list is your Daily Habit and Ritual List. This is for activities you need to practice to improve (or at the very least maintain) on a regular basis. These repeating items should not be cluttering up your main to-do lists. These need to be isolated and monitored in a different way. The items going onto this list are often the most important things in your life – planning your day, reviewing your goals, updating your lists, exercise, drinking eight glasses of water, eating your five-a-day, balancing your bank account, date night with your partner… We looked at this subject inside the Balance Pillar and will come back to it again in the Tracking Pillar, but just as a quick pointer, this is the list that is broken down into the critical areas of your life you need to master on a regular basis:

- Health
- Finance
- Relationships

- Emotions
- Personal Development
- Life Management

Make a list of two or three things that support your growth in each of these categories and that you are committed to doing on a daily or at least a weekly basis.

Again, Daily Life Tracker ® focuses very much on this area and I am not aware of any other effective way of doing it.

3) Calendar

My best advice for your calendar is 'Keep it Simple'. Your calendar should be restricted to scheduling meetings or events that have a fixed date and time to them. You can also use it for booking time for yourself when you do not want anyone disturbing you. Do not get caught out by putting your to-do list into your calendar or diary. We all know that life can take over and items you want to do today will not get done. If they are in your calendar, you have to keep on rolling them from one day to the next and this can be very demoralising.

Checklists

Checklists are a magnificent way of taking control. You understand that there is a situation you may come across in the future, such as travelling abroad. It is often easier to think through a situation when you are not in the midst of it. How many times have you forgotten something you should have done or taken with you? There really is no excuse for this. A simple checklist can make sure everything goes with you, every time. And if there is something you miss off the list initially, make sure it goes on the list for next time. Once is a mistake, twice or more and it starts to become a problem. A holiday checklist may be obvious, and we may all have one, but the same principle applies to many other areas of your life. With the huge complexity in all areas of our lives comes the undeniable need for planning and checklists. This is how we achieve MASTERY in all we do.

Back to getting intimate...

Now you understand the structure of the lists I propose you keep, we can get back to understanding why you need to spend 20 minutes a day getting intimate with them. You should spend this time with no particular goal in mind. Just look at the lists, absorb them and make adjustments and additions as they come to you. Here are the sorts of things you should be thinking about during the review:

- Make sure the way you have categorised your Master List makes sense.
- Re-categorise your lists.
- Consolidate actions and outcomes.
- Make sure your Daily Action List relates to your weekly outcomes.
- Make sure your weekly outcomes take you towards your goals and are appropriate to where you are at the moment.
- Regularly reassess your daily habits and rituals for appropriateness.

Getting up close and intimate with your lists every day will give you confidence in your system. Confidence that whenever anything hits your desk, you know exactly where to place it, making you much more effective in processing anything that comes your way. It also makes you much more efficient at managing your planned work. If you do not trust the system, you will not use it and all your hard work will be wasted. The constant review of your lists, done at least on a weekly basis, will ensure that you build this trust and with it your success.

Goals

Goal setting is one of the most powerful exercises you can go through. Much has been asserted over the years about the value of written goals. It really stands to reason that if you know where you want to go and can clearly express it then you have much more chance of achieving success than if you just wander around waiting to trip over it. Rarely does a good idea interrupt you. You need to plan for it and make it happen.

There is an infamous study of Harvard graduates that suggests that only 3% of the graduating year had written down their goals and 20 years later these 3% had a net worth in excess of the other 97% put together. It seems that this story may be apocryphal but I still believe that the principle is a valid hypothesis. The main point here is that by writing down your goals, you create a clarity around what you want to get out of life. With clarity comes the ability to focus on doing whatever it takes to achieve those results. It also fires off your reticular activating system. This means that your subconscious mind is looking out for things that will help you to achieve your goals without you consciously thinking about it. It is like the day you decide to buy a new car and then all of a sudden you see that car everywhere you look. The cars were always there, but now your mind is on high alert to spot them as they now mean something to you.

To power up this idea of written goals helping you to achieve your dreams, you should re-write them every night before you go to bed and every morning when you get up. This way they are always at the forefront of your mind and when any opportunity to make progress towards their attainment shows itself, you are ready to take that chance. To the untrained eye, this might look like luck or the universe, but in reality it is simply awareness of what was always there.

There are essentially two types of goals. Goals you can achieve, tick off and move on from, such as buying your dream home or a new car. Then there are goals that are long term and can never really be ticked off as done. These might include weight loss goals or life balance. Yes, of course, you can tick this goal off as completed from an 'achievement of the numbers' point of view, but for this to really make a difference to your life, you need to maintain this goal and make sure you stay at this target weight and not let things slip backwards because you have lost focus. This is where Daily Life Tracker ® really comes into its own.

When you go through the Goal Setting programme, you first need to go through a brainstorming process of bringing forth as many goal ideas as possible to get you thinking big and creatively. Whilst it is important in this process to set some smaller goals you can achieve quite quickly, it is also critical to set some big audacious goals that will really challenge you. It is often just as difficult to achieve a small goal as it is to achieve a big one, so why not think big.

You then need to narrow these goals down into a small number of short term, life changing goals that you can be confident of achieving.

Following this, you must put the rubber to the road and turn these dreams into clear action plans with milestones along the way to make sure you are on track with your efforts. With determination and persistence, you can achieve any goal you set out to achieve as long as you are willing to pay the price. However, most people are not truly willing to pay the price. They look at the surface of what others have achieved and think that since everyone else had it so easy, they should also have it easy. The truth is that it is never easy. When you are looking at anyone else's achievements, you are just seeing the tip of the iceberg and you do not see all the blood, sweat and tears that went into that person's dreams. There is always a price to pay. The questions is, are you willing to pay it?

It is worth stopping here for a moment to think about the action plan that will take you to the goal you have set. You need to create what I would call a Critical Path. This is essentially a series of milestones that start out at the point when the goal is achieved and count back to the current date. If you want to achieve your goal in 12 months, set a specific date 12 months from now when it MUST be done. Then think about what needs to have happened in nine months if that final deadline is to be achieved. Do the same for six months and three months. Next, you can get into a little more detail about what needs to be done this month, this week and then today. The closer the timeframe, the more detailed the action list needs to be. You need clarity in order to take action. If you don't know exactly what you are going to do next and how it fits into the overall plan, then you are unlikely to get started.

I have often found that if I leave a bridge back to the past, I will never truly invest myself fully in my future goals. One of the best ways to move forwards is to burn all your bridges because if there are no other options you will always find a way.

It is sometimes helpful to let other people know about your goals so they will keep you accountable. We all have someone in our lives who is very happy to let us know when we are not following through with what we said. These people can be a real pain in the arse, but they are the best people to have on board so you can prove to them that you are up to it.

And while this is a pretty obvious statement, it is still worth making.

Until you have dealt with your current goals, you are not able to create and move on to new ones, and it is in these new and ever growing goals that you will find your true, incredible self.

Today I will do what others won't, so tomorrow I can accomplish what others can't.
(Jerry Rice)

While goal setting is very powerful, there are a couple of things we need to understand to get the very most out of these efforts:

- Goals alone will not motivate you into action. For that, you need to build habits that when combined with self-reflection and flexibility lead to better and better habits.
- As Jim Rohn said, "Goals are not about what you get. Goals are about who you become in the pursuit of what you get.".

To help in this process, I have created a real-time Goal Setting Workshop and Workbook that will change your life forever. Go to our online resources at www.productivitypowerhouse.info/goal-setting-workshop. You can get access for free as a thank you for taking the time to read my book.

Efficiency and Time Saving

I will end this Pillar with a series of additional quick fire efficiency hacks that will help your day move more efficiently.

Invest Your Time

The best way for you to create more time for yourself in the future is to invest it now. If you invest your time in the following activities it will pay back many times over in the future.

1. Train other people to do some of the stuff you do not really need

to do yourself.

   a. If a job takes you five minutes a day and it takes you one hour to train someone else to do it, a lot of people would dismiss this as being a waste of time. But after 12 days, your time is paid back and it is all gain after that. Your time is your most valuable commodity. Every five minutes you can save each day is worth every little bit of effort it takes to get there. Be a master and save every minute you can.

2. Automate as much of what you do as possible.

   a. Technology is moving forward at a frightening rate and you need to take advantage of it. Anything that has a repetitive nature about it can be automated and it will be worth whatever time and money it takes to get you there. Be careful that you are not chasing shiny pennies all the time. You need to be thoughtful about it, but your imagination is really your only limit here. If you can automate your activities, you are freed up to be more creative – which is the stuff that machines are not so good at.

3. Set up systems.

   a. Even if you cannot automate something, you may be able to set up a system that takes some of the thought out of the process. If you can remove the thought then you remove some of the friction and therefore generate more time. Also, once you have a system, it is much easier to pass the process on to someone else, who you can train to do it.

4. Outsource whatever you can.

   a. This simply means finding other people, inside or outside of your business or home, to do these things for you.

Outsourcing is a big enough issue to demand its own section (see below).

The problem is that many people feel like they are too busy to invest this time. This is very short-termist and will make things much more difficult for you when you want to grow and expand your business. Taking the time to do this now means you are INVESTING and not simply spending time.

Outsourcing

As mentioned above, this is really another way of investing your time, but this is worthy of further comment.

You can pretty much outsource anything you do if you give enough thought to it. This is the basis of the four hour work week that Tim Ferriss talks about. If you can outsource everything you do, your job becomes a management role where you just need to keep the plates spinning.

The biggest issue with outsourcing is making sure that the time you save is effectively used. By this I mean that if you pay a gardener £20 per hour to mow your lawn, then you can build your business and generate £100 or more with that hour you saved. However, if you are going to pay the gardener £20 per hour to mow your lawn so you can waste it watching some stupid TV show, then you are just wasting money.

The next big question is when should you start to outsource? This is really interesting as I have never come across any entrepreneur who said that they outsourced too soon. I am sure there are some, but for the most part we tend to do this much later than we really should. The reason people tend to set up outsourcing operations too late is that they think they cannot afford it. Initially, this may appear to be true, but the reality is that you have probably just not applied enough thought to the situation. As I mentioned before, this is really a matter of comparative value and if you can generate more than you spend then you must do it.

Further, bringing in outsourcers at an early stage can actually create more opportunities within your business and help you to grow much faster. A few months ago, a colleague of mine, Darren, was looking for a job. I had a role within the business that I needed someone to do but I thought I could not afford to employ someone full time to do it. But the opportunity was there and it would not be there for long. In fact, he had just asked me to provide him with a reference for another job. I decided to jump in with both feet and offered him the full time role of Technical Director of Productivity Powerhouse. There was a lot of work to do, but it was not instantly income generating. That is, until I employed him. As soon as I did this, it opened up a new arm to our business and we now offer IT Technical Support and Development Services to third parties, and this part of the business is growing really well. Had I not gone for it, I would still be struggling for someone I could trust with my own internal development role and a good chunk of my current business would not exist. Only four months later, I am faced with a similar question – the outsourcing operation that I use to produce my mobile apps is asking if I will commit to giving them a consistent work programme so they can hire three dedicated developers for Productivity Powerhouse. The answer has to be yes, but only as soon as they have proved themselves with the work I have already given them.

This takes me on to the next point, which is trust. When you set on an outsourcer, you need to do your due diligence. This means making sure they will do a good job. Most outsourcing operations will provide you with references and testimonials from other organisations they have done work for. It is really important to follow up on this. If they do a bad job, even if you don't end up paying them, you will have wasted an awful lot of time.

So, make your decision based on a thorough background check and not simply on cost. We all want to get a good deal but cheapest is not always best. In fact, it is not often best. They say that if you want 'Cheap, Fast and Good', you can get any two of these but never all three.

Once you have chosen your outsourcer, this is where the fun starts. Seriously, this can be a lot of fun. After all, you are getting stuff done, but you are not actually doing it. So what is the trick to getting a good job done by your outsourcers? Apart from the selection process, the biggest key to getting what you want is clarity. The more detailed and clear the brief you provide, the more chance you have of getting what you want. This will be more work up front but, as always, the time spent planning the work will pay dividends many times over.

Then you need to manage the process. Don't think you can just leave them to get on with it, no matter how good they are. You need to have regular meetings to make sure that targets are being met and goals and milestones are on track. The more frequent your meetings, the better. I have found that our projects have moved forward much more effectively if we have video calls with our outsourcers every other day or even every day. In doing this, the outsourcer knows they need to make good progress each day but they also know that if they have any questions they don't have to spend lots of time trying to second guess what you might want. Healthy communication is a major plus for both parties.

Now, if you get all of this right: you go through a rigorous selection process, you provide a clear brief and you manage the process properly, you will start to build a relationship with your outsourcer.

This is likely to lead to them giving you priority of resource, both in terms of quality and speed, because they know how you operate and that you are a repeat buyer. This relationship is why my outsourcers are coming to me offering to engage people to purely work on my projects. This is very powerful.

Remember that the best outsourcing arrangements come from a win-win situation. If either party feels like they have been mistreated then issues are going to arise that will detract from the work that is being done and can seriously damage both parties. No-one is going to come out on top in a public online battle. Apart from the public embarrassment that is caused, it is also a massive distraction which drains your energy. So make sure you build a good relationship and if the worst comes to the worst and things to go sour, which they can, then conduct your negotiations in private.

Delegation

It is very important that you learn to delegate tasks effectively. This is very similar to outsourcing and teaching people what you do, which I have mentioned above, but I tend to think of this as more of an internal process within your own organisation. Any time you ask someone else to do something, this is a delegation process. All the lessons of relationship and clarity I discussed within the Outsourcing section apply equally here.

Management

While training, delegation and outsourcing pass some of the workload onto other people, it does not pass the responsibility. That is not strictly true, I suppose, as you do need to hold those people to account for what they do, but the point I am making is that you cannot just leave them to it. You need to manage the process as it is ultimately your head on the line if things don't work out. If you outsource your marketing and no business comes in, it is you that goes out of business, no matter how justified you are in your complaints about your marketer.

The best way to handle this is through your Waiting For list, which would fit within the context structure of the lists we discussed previously. Every task or project you outsource goes onto your Waiting For list which you should review every couple of days so you can follow up as appropriate. Every time you have a follow up call with your outsourcer or the person you have delegated a task or project to you need to go in with a clear goal for the call and you need to end the call with a clear way forward for the person working for you.

One word of warning – do not micro-manage! The purpose of keeping track of all of these things on your Waiting For list is because you need to know that progress is being made. You do not need to manage the detail. If you have detailed action lists behind every project you are waiting for someone to do, you are overthinking things. Get rid of all of the detailed actions and trust that your team can cope. You will be surprised at how much you are not really needed! I have experienced big picture managers and micro-managers and I will tell you without any fear of contradiction that the big picture managers win out every time, if for no other reason than the fact that the people working for them feel trusted and empowered.

Team Building

Everyone that you work with throughout your day is part of your team. Some of these people will be internal to your organisation and some will be third parties. Whoever they are they need to be nurtured and made to feel like their contribution is important. Always remember to say thank you to your team for their efforts. And there is nothing more satisfying to your key players than keeping them informed and well briefed about what you are doing and where the business is going.

Networking

"Your network is your net worth!" Have you ever heard that phrase? Well, it is true. And I'll let you into a secret, I hate networking. But just because I don't like something does not mean that I should not do it. In fact, all successful people have a bunch of things they hate doing, but they do them anyway. That is what makes them successful.

Not all networking is equal. I have been to some good networking meetings and some very bad ones. The worst ones for me are those where everyone turns up to sell and nothing else. I know that our businesses all depend on sales but when everyone just turns up to sell then no-one wins and you end up wasting two hours of your life.

The best networking events are those where there is a little education plus everyone in the room is looking to help each other out. When this happens, the world opens up. If you get the right people in the room all looking out for each other, it is incredible what can happen. But remember, it takes two to tango. If only one party is following up and the other is just there for the ride, and to take what they can, then the relationship will be very short-lived.

Mentors, Coaches and Peers

A good mentor can knock years off your training and development. We can all muddle through using trial and error, but if you really want to accelerate the process you need to find someone who has been there and done it. The knowledge you gain from someone else's experience is without question one of the greatest gifts you can ever receive. A good mentor knows what you are going through and can help you avoid the pitfalls they experienced. This does not mean you will never make any mistakes. Mistakes are an opportunity for growth and if you are not willing to fail you will never make progress. But if someone can help you avoid the mistakes they made and speed things up by taking chances you might not have considered, you really must take advantage.

Whilst a mentor has been through whatever you are going through, a coach is there to observe what you are doing from a distance as it is often not easy to see what you might be doing wrong because you are too close to the situation. They say that you cannot see yourself from inside the frame. A coach does not need to have 'been there and got the t-shirt', they just need to have the skills to observe what you are doing and help you correct yourself. Tiger Woods was the greatest golfer of his time but he still had a coach to observe his swing, which he could not see while he was in the middle of it.

Asking for help is not a weakness, it is a strength as it shows your willingness to learn and your desire to speed things up.

Jim Rohn said that your income will be the average of the five people who you spend most time with. I am not sure whether the numbers are right, but the principle is very valid. You will tend to modulate to those around you, so if you mix with people who are getting shit done then you will not want to be left behind and you will raise your game. You want to get into the presence of people who are really shaking things up and making a difference, and then try to lead them to even bigger highs. You must always keep raising the game.

Who you spend time with is who you become.
(Tony Robbins)

Saving Minutes to Make Hours

They say that every little helps. This is certainly true of your time. Most people go through their lives in a dazed state where they are merely going through the motions. If you can teach yourself to be more thoughtful or mindful in everything you do, you will be surprised at how much time you can save and put to better use. As we discussed in the Habit Pillar, our brains like to go on to autopilot. This is a very powerful mechanism that if it were not in place would make our lives very difficult. But the counter to that is that when we are not mindful of what we are doing, some of those habits do not serve us. Constantly try to figure out how to do things better or faster or more efficiently. If you can save a minute or two on each thing you do, you will soon have an extra hour, or even two, that you can put to better use.

This is where the rest of the book comes into play because no matter how much time you might save, if you then go on to use it on wasteful pursuits, it was all for nothing.

Say No!

This is the simplest and most powerful way of controlling your time. Just say no a little more often. Because so many of us want to be helpful and because we get excited about new ventures, we can find ourselves overloaded with stuff that actually does not have much value to us. Remember, there are only 168 hours in a week. Whatever you say yes to means that you are saying no to something else. Not only does this detract from your own life, but it also means you are ultimately going to be letting people down, either with the quality of your work because you cannot give 100% effort to so many things or simply because you will never be able to get everything done and you will miss deadlines and meetings and become the person that no-one can rely upon.

The real trick is knowing what to say no to. You cannot say no to everything because if you do, people will stop asking you and you will miss some great opportunities. What do you say yes or no to? This is down to your judgement. You will make some good calls and some bad calls; you just need to make sure you learn from every one so that next time you are more on the mark.

Declutter

One of your biggest distractions by far is the clutter you hold throughout your life. I am a bit of a neat freak, I will admit, and sometimes I need to let go in order to live in the real world with a real family! However, as far as your personal productivity goes, nothing will slow you down more than the distraction of clutter. So if you feel like things are not in order, do yourself a massive favour and declutter your life in every sense:

- Office
- Desk
- House
- Email
- Car
- Your head
- Anything and everything else

Whether it is physical stuff you need to deal with or all the stuff going on inside your head or the digital information you hold and that keeps expanding out of all sense of proportion, you need to take stock, come up with a better system and make the changes. Depending on how chaotic your life is, this may take you quite some time, but when it is done this is like a mental shower and you will feel the stress fall away.

Stop Double-Dipping

If at all possible, only touch things once. This is, of course, not always possible. If something is going to take you less than two or three minutes, it is not worth the time it will take you to add it to your list, so get it done right away. Everything else needs to go onto your lists. Other than the two or three minute jobs, we will always touch everything at least twice – once to get it on the list and at least once to do it. When you go back to one of your actions and you start the doing process, stick with it until you are done. This tip alone will make the world of difference to everything you do. So often, we stop just short of completion, maybe out of boredom, maybe because we don't quite know how to finish, maybe because we are being a perfectionist. Then when we pick it back up later we take a long time to get back to where we left off because we are now out of flow. This is a real progress killer. Just get it done. Only then can you move on to the next thing. If you are leaving open loops at the end of the day, you still have to come back to them the next day and the promise of what you could do tomorrow remains unrealised.

Some projects, of course, cannot be completed in one sitting, no matter how determined you are. Writing this book is a great example. For big projects like this, you need to break them down into timeframes or chunks of work and then stick at that until it is done. In fact, as I sit here today it is 10:45pm and I have committed to myself that I am not going to go to bed until this Pillar is complete. There is still a lot of work to do, but this is the only way to get it finished.

Do Your Thinking Once

Thinking is hard work, so don't do it any more often than you need to. This means you should always create a plan, create an order priority so you know exactly what you are going to do next, plan your day the night before so when you get up in the morning you are immediately ready to get going, create empowering habits and build systems and automation to make your life easier.

Email Mastery

Email is one of those things that we cannot seem to get away from. It can be a great drain on your time if you do not manage it properly. You can go into all sorts of detail with this, setting up rules and automation, but it is really just a matter of filtering and filing. The key things to consider are:

- Get your inbox to zero at the end of every day.
- Unsubscribe to anything that you don't want to see.
- Set up a series of folders to quickly move your emails into so you can clear your inbox down. Mine are:
    - To-Do (Urgent)
    - To-Do (When You Have Time)
    - To-Do (Waiting)
    - To-Do (Read)
    - Archive
- Create a few quick steps in the header of your email platform so you can quickly process all your emails into these folders as they come in.
- Regularly review these key folders.

Until I was recently coached by Martin Perry of Taming Your Inbox,

I used to have a huge number of folders that I processed my emails into. This was much more time consuming than having one Archive folder. For the amount of times I look back at old emails, the single Archive folder and the email search functionality is more than adequate for my needs and saves me loads of time every day.

Build your Mobile Lifestyle

Technology is progressing faster than you could ever imagine, and the common analogy is that we are now all walking around with more computer processing power in our pockets than it took to land a man on the moon. With this level of mobility, why would you want to spend all your time in the office? If you could be sitting on a beach making calls, placing orders, video chatting with clients, why wouldn't you? Today's mobile technology, more than ever before, gives us the freedom to run our businesses 24/7/365 from anywhere in the world. And if you can work the whole-life balance idea into every day of your life, wouldn't you rather do that than try to get 48 weeks of work to balance with four weeks of vacation? That does not seem like much of a balance at all.

Do Meetings Right

Meetings don't need to be avoided. They just need to be managed properly:

- Have a clear outcome for the meeting.
- Always go in with a clear agenda.
- If you can do the meeting in five minutes, do it in five minutes and don't get caught out thinking that you need to fill an hour to make the meeting worthwhile.
- Manage the meeting and keep people on task.

- Make sure you come out of the meeting with a series of next actions that are clearly assigned to individuals.
- Always take notes.
- Have someone in the meeting who produces an action focused set of minutes – these should be distributed within 24 hours of the meeting.

Focus – One Thing Thinking

Earlier in the book, I talked about how improving your energy levels would give you the biggest bang for your buck as far as personal productivity goes. That being the case, laser-like FOCUS on one single activity is by far the **fastest bang for your buck**.

One Thing Thinking means you are entirely focused on a single activity and it works across many timeframes:

- What is the one thing you need to get done this minute?
- What is the one thing you need to get done in the next hour?
- What is the one thing you need to get done this morning?
- What is the one thing you need to get done today?
- What is the one thing you need to get done this week?
- What is the one thing you need to get done this month?
- What is the one thing you need to get done this quarter?
- What is the one thing you need to get done this year?

The main thing, is to keep the main thing, the main thing.
(Stephen Covey)

Stop Multi-Tasking

Many people wear the multi-tasking label as a badge of honour, but in reality this is not a good thing. Multi-tasking is one of the worst productivity ideas that you will ever come across. Studies have shown that the stop-start nature of multi-tasking throughout your day significantly affects the processing power of your brain. Obviously, no-one is ever going to focus 100% of their time on a single exercise for a long period of time, but the closer you can get to this principle the better. We saw earlier in the book that there is a great power in setting 90 minutes aside to get yourself focused on your ONE thing, but when you string a series of these together you start to really make things happen.

What about the Real World?

Having talked extensively about the power of focus, planning and staying on task, we still need to live in the real world where we have chores and small jobs that can never be related to your life goals or purpose or even your weekly outcomes. But they still need to be done. I have found that the best way to deal with these things is to give them their own time. I call this Keep Up Time as it is the time when I am keeping up with all the niggling bits and pieces that need my attention.

Firstly, you can outsource some of these things.

However, this is not always possible and sometimes it can be a nice break to get away from the big stuff for ten minutes and do something that requires no brain power at all.

In my experience, these administrative-type tasks can play on your mind and distract you from your bigger goals. The problem I found was that these distractions would be constant because there is always something that needs my attention. The best way I have found to deal with this is to set specific Keep Up Time aside three times a day in order to get these things done. Depending on how much there is to do, this might be three lots of 20 minutes or it could be anything up to three whole hours, but I try not to let it go beyond that. I tend to time these things around 10am, 3pm and 7pm. The idea is that if I know that I have time set aside for these things then I do not need to give them any attention at all during the rest of the day. And since I have these blocks of time set for morning, afternoon and evening, I always know I have the opportunity to deal with this stuff during the day, no matter how urgent it is.

The sort of things that I cover in Keep Up Time are:

- Planning
- Phone calls
- Accounts
- Email
- Mail
- Tidying desk
- House chores
- Etc...

Keep Up or Catch Up

You have two choices – Keep up or catch up.

For most people, they are constantly in catch up mode where they feel like they need to freeze time in order to just get themselves straight. All the things you keep putting off weigh heavily on your mind and your stress levels build and build until you can hardly stand yourself. The worst thing that catch up mode creates is regret because of all the things you miss out on when you can't move forward.

If you do fall behind and need to catch up, you have three options:

1) Just do it

Sometimes you have to bite the bullet and just do it, employing some of the techniques outlined in this book. This might apply to something like your taxes that you have left until the last minute.

2) Reset

Some things you can just reset and start again. For example, if you said you would exercise more by running two miles every other day and you have not done it for the last four weeks, then you don't need to be going out and running 28 miles to catch up.

3) Create a catch up plan

Sometimes you need to figure out what you have missed and then schedule it in for the next few days to get back on track. For example, if you set yourself the goal of writing one page of a book every day for 100 days and you missed the last ten days, you need to create a plan to get you back in line. So, for the next ten days you do two pages per day until you have recovered your lost time.

On the other hand, if you can train yourself to be more disciplined and keep up with everything that is going on in your life, then this builds self-esteem and confidence that you are in control of things and can take on the world. You feel like you are consistent in your demands on yourself and it feels great.

Organisational Tools

Now we are starting to get into the specific strategies for becoming more productive, we also need to start thinking about the tools that can help the process. Of course, tools are just tools. No matter how good they are, they are all useless unless you use them. But when used appropriately, they are fantastic at helping you to organise yourself most effectively.

Organisational tools cover a myriad of things: you may prefer the tactile touch of pen and paper or you may prefer the single input efficiency of the latest technology. The tools, in and of themselves, do not really matter. What matters is how you use them. If you try to force yourself to use something that doesn't feel right, you are never going to get very much out of it because it jars against your nature.

Where should you keep your lists?

There is no fixed answer to this question, of course. It is entirely up to you as an individual. Some people are technophobes and would never trust computer software to maintain such important information. Some people need to work on paper otherwise it doesn't feel real. Everyone has their own personal preferences. For me, it has to be on a computer. I cannot bear the inefficiency of having to rewrite my lists over and over. I could use the time I would spend rewriting my lists to gain a greater degree of clarity over the lists and processes themselves. Others would say that the tactile use of a pen to rewrite your lists helps your brain to process the tasks better as you reclarify the significance and relevance of each item. You need to understand the way you work and weigh up the pros and cons according to your own style.

Pillar 4 – INTEGRATION

Gathering Your Thoughts

One of the first things you need to do is gather your ideas together and get them out of your head, so having an effective way of doing this is very important.

Voice recorders are fabulous for longer thoughts and notes and nowadays these come with every smartphone. Voice recognition software is also getting much better, so converting these notes into text that is more useable is much easier than it used to be.

There are also many smartphone apps that allow you to take notes on the go. The real trick here is to make sure you use these tools appropriately so the action or idea goes to its most appropriate storage point as quickly as possible and does not just become another chore.

No matter where I go I carry a small notepad in my pocket. I have one that fits in my wallet, which is fantastic, but I have also sourced some five-in-one notepads that include a small pad of paper, two different types of post-it notes and a pen with a small stylus on the end. I am finding this a wonderful addition to my toolkit.

Filing Systems

There are essentially two types of filing system – electronic (scanning) or paper. Whilst I will always go with technology for my organisational and list building systems, I am still old school when it comes to storing documents. I am sure that some people will swear by scanning documents into a system so they can be accessed anywhere in the world, but personally I have never found the process to be fluid enough to beat a good paper filing system. And this is really the key point. Whatever method you decide to go with, you need to make sure it is efficient. Any piece of paper that hits my desk can be filed in less than 30 seconds – and testing this is always a lot of fun.

I got my filing system from David Allen. It is super simple, but a little counterintuitive. Everything is stored alphabetically in A4 cardboard folders. Don't be tempted to group projects together as this will actually make your system more complex. With a single alphabetical system, it is very clear where everything goes.

To make this work, the most important thing is an index. This is a simple log of all the folders so you can easily search for anything you may need. Trust is critical with any system, so you must make sure that whenever you add a folder to your system you add it to the index. As soon as you lose trust in the system, you will stop using it and all that hard work will have gone to waste.

This does take some time to set up, but I have found that once it is there and in place, it is by far the fastest and most efficient way for me to operate.

As I am writing this part of the book I am sure that it will become out of date very shortly as scanning devices and automatic filing systems improve and become more commonplace. The principles of having a system that is easy to use and access remain the same, so these are not wasted words even though they may soon be outdated.

One further problem with the paper system is that eventually you are going to run out of space, so it is important that you archive or destroy old files once in a while.

In-Tray Systems

I use a five in-tray system to look after any documents I need for work that I am currently working on. These are:

- **In-tray**
    - Whenever anything enters my office, this is where it goes. Simple. This tray should be empty by the end of the day.
- **Urgent**
    - Anything that needs attention today goes into this tray. This tray should be empty by the end of the day.
- **Small Projects**
    - Any project that can be completed within an hour or two goes here.
- **Large Projects**
    - You guessed it. Any project that will take longer than an hour or so (of focused time) goes into this tray.
- **Waiting For**
    - Once I have worked on something and leveraged it out to someone else then the documents go here. This way I know that someone else has these projects in hand.

Any document or project I am not currently working on goes into the reference filing system I mentioned above so I always know where to find it.

Once again, the key to this system is to operate it consistently and make sure you review it on a regular basis.

Tickler System

This is another brilliant system I learned from David Allen and it is incredibly effective. You should think of the Tickler System as a diary where you can store physical papers, such as a bill that needs to be paid at the end of the month. The Tickler System is made up of 12 monthly folders for each month of the year and 31 daily folders for each day of the current month.

At the beginning of January, the 31 daily folders sit at the front of the stack with the 12 monthly folders behind in order. Any papers that need to be dealt with on a particular date in January go into any of those 31 folders. Anything that needs to be dealt with later in the year goes into one of the 12 monthly folders. On the second of January you will move the folder marked 1st to sit behind the February folder, and this process continues each day until all 31 of the daily folders are sitting behind the February monthly folder. You then take all the papers from the February monthly folder and allocate them into the individual days. This continues throughout the year. This may sound a little complex at first, but once you physically start to use it you will see how effective it is at managing paperwork and physical items that only become relevant at a later date.

Other Tools

Aside from the obvious productivity tools that I have just discussed, one thing I have found to be oddly powerful is the use of 'nice stuff'. For some reason, when you choose quality tools, you enjoy using them more and therefore get drawn towards the activities they promote.

I love pens! I don't know why, but I do, and I have all sorts of them for all sorts of occasions. They don't have to be expensive, but they have to be something unique or have quality about them. I have two favourites. The first is my multi-purpose Cross pen which has three colours and a pencil. I use this all the time because the multiple colours allow me to highlight things as I am writing, which really helps with my note taking. The second was a real revelation to me and it is what I call my Write by Night™ pen. It has a light in the nib of the pen which means I can write in the dark. Whilst I never sleep with my phone in the bedroom, I always sleep with a pad of paper next to my bed because I find that lots of my best ideas come to me in the middle of the night or when I wake up first thing in the morning. Having a pad of paper next to the bed means I can capture those ideas and then go straight back to sleep without worrying about whether I will forget them when I get up. Flicking the night light on all the time would disturb my wife, which is not good for a harmonious marriage, but when I discovered my Write by Night™ pen, this was a game changer.

The 5 Pillars in Action

Keep a distraction log.

- Make sure you know what the ONE THING is that you should be focused on.
- Throughout the day, make a note of ANYTHING that distracts you from that ONE THING.
- Make a note of WHEN you get distracted.
- Note how you react to the distractions.
- Note how long it takes you to get back into your flow.
- See if you can spot any patterns that will help you stay more focused in the future.

Pillar 5 –
TRACKING

Pillar 5 – TRACKING

By now, you should have mastered the foundational skills you need to be at your most productive and understand the strategies that these foundations support. The final step is to make sure that all of this effort is not wasted by drifting back into old habits. To do this, you need to track your progress and consistently operate your new found skills. This is a conditioning process, which means that if you master and apply these skills now, they will stay with you forever.

The only reason for us to measure and track anything is so we can grow. How can you ever improve on anything unless you know how you are doing? How can you be sure that you have made progress unless you have a method of measuring where you were, where you are now and where you want to be? Measurement interrupts your habitual patterns and brings the issues from the subconscious mind into the conscious mind. The more frequently and precisely the monitoring, the better.

What gets measured gets done. What does not get measured gets missed.
(Peter Drucker)

In my opinion tracking and measuring is the precursor to growth or any worthwhile change. If you want to get your finances under control, track everything you earn and spend. If you want to lose weight, track everything that passes your lips. If you want to take control over your time, track how you are spending your time over the period of a few days.

If you want to improve any area of your life, you need to work at it. During the journey, things are going to get tough and from one day to the next your results are likely to be imperceptible. When this is happening, you want to have a system that demonstrates you are moving in the right direction and gives you the encouragement to keep going. If you can track your progress day by day, you can start to see the small changes and you will be spurred on to keep going.

The real trick is not to just track things. You need to analyse what is going on and look for patterns. You see, it's all about pattern recognition. The more you track, the more patterns you will start to see. And when you start to spot the patterns in the things you do and the results you get from the things you do, you are in a far better position to change the patterns you don't like.

I believe that Daily Logging is the key to big time success.
(Stu Mittleman, Former World Champion and World Record Holder, Ultrarunning Hall of Fame)

Tracking your actions is a really interesting and powerful process as it helps you to spot patterns. As I discussed in the Habit Pillar earlier in the book, much of what we do is born out of habit and we are often unaware that it is happening as we just drift through the day in a daze. In order to track what is going on in your life most effectively, you need to be much more mindful of your actions. This fact itself will reduce the amount of times you actually succumb to the distractions because you know they are not serving you and so you stop.

The action of measurement and tracking, not only allows you to observe the patterns you are operating throughout your day, but it also serves to correct some of those destructive patterns. Bringing this awareness into your conscious mind makes it easier and more likely that you will stop giving in to the distractions, even though it will not stop the distraction from occurring. This in itself also serves you because now you start to feel that you are in control of those irritating interruptions that happen throughout the day. The email will still come in, the phone will still ring, the TV show will still start, the Facebook post will still appear, but you will mindfully ignore them and continue to pursue the important task you have in hand.

Pillar 5 – TRACKING

A friend of mine, James, is in the middle of an interesting experiment. If you saw James you would not think that he is overweight at all, but he feels that this body fat percentage is too high and he wants a stronger and healthier body that will give him the energy to enjoy his family more than ever before. James has been working with a personal trainer who has been asking him to record everything he eats. James, being James has gone to town on this. He is recording every single gramme and every single calorie that passes his lips. And this is having a dramatic effect. He is losing weight and body fat, but more importantly he is becoming much more health conscious and aware of the good and bad things that were impacting upon his energy levels.

Some very obvious benefits result from the recording process itself, however the real life changing benefits come from what you do with this information. The goal of tracking is not just to give you some interesting data. The goal is to improve your life. The insights are great as they give you a base to work from, but you can only improve if you do something about it by changing the way you do things.

But beware of false patterns. Sometimes your results do not reflect your efforts, but don't let this dissuade you from recording what is going on. There are still patterns in there that you have perhaps not found. Short term results can be misleading and you may need to take multiple measurements to figure out what is going on. Don't let this frustrate you. This is exciting. When you start to see patterns and figure out solutions, you are on your way to finding some real gold. Often the key is a little more consistency. You need to trust that the power of layering one action on top of another will get you to your desired outcome. Unless you are measuring what is going on, you are going to miss these clues.

So, what are the main things that result from you tracking just one area of your life in detail?

1) It makes you more mindful and acutely aware of everything you are doing in the area you are tracking.

2) You can start to do more of the right things.

3) You get disturbed by the things you are doing that are not congruent with the person you want to be or see yourself as.

4) It interrupts the habitual patterns you were unaware of as your subconscious mind has cleverly camouflaged them from right in front of you.

5) It improves your understanding of how you operate, giving you the chance to make changes.

6) You start to study the subject more because you start to see interesting patterns that you can improve on.

7) When you start to spot patterns and create systems you are able to help others get the same results.

8) It wakes you up to other areas of your life that may need to be tracked and monitored in order to improve them. Examples of areas of your life that may benefit from tracking might be:

    a. Diet

    b. Time management

    c. Exercise

    d. Distractions

    e. Money

f. Family and relationship time

g. Personal development

h. Work (via key performance indicators)

i. In fact, any area of your life can be tracked and improved with a little thought and imagination.

The Irony of Tracking

Ironically, you will be happy to track the good things you are doing in your life, but you will get very uncomfortable tracking the bad things. But most gain is made from this process when you track and therefore interrupt the bad patterns.

One Thing at a Time

If you want to make real lasting changes to any area of your life, you should make a study of it. If you think back to your school days and doing experiments in a science lesson, you were taught that in order to establish a credible result you can only change one thing at a time. The experiment needs to be controlled so you know the change that is having the effect. If you change too many things in one go, you have no idea which one created the outcome you now observe. So you change one thing and track its results. Then you change another thing and track its results. And you continue to do this until you are happy with where you have taken the experiment.

So, treat yourself like a test laboratory. Theory is great but it is no substitute for hard cold facts that come from trying things out. Test, test, test and test again. Now, don't be stupid, of course, and start to harm yourself by testing ridiculous notions, you need to apply common sense, but the proof of the pudding is in the eating, so have a try.

Feedback Loop

One of the master secrets to making progress in anything you do is getting feedback. However, feedback is of limited use unless it is instant and clear to understand.

The faster the feedback, the better. In fact, slow feedback helps to drive bad habits and addictions. One of the great failings of our society is that everyone is looking for short term instant gratification. People who smoke know that it is not good for them, but they want the instant buzz that the cigarette gives them even though they know it is killing them. The true impact of smoking comes many years down the line when it is often too late to do anything about it. If smoking a cigarette was going to kill you as soon as you put it to your lips, no-one would ever do it, but because the feedback from that cigarette comes slowly, people don't care and so they continue to do it.

If feedback comes late, it is difficult to remember exactly what you did, and it is often too late to do anything about it.

I will share with you a personal example of how this has affected me. Throughout my life, I have always been very healthy and never been into hospital. That is until about four years ago. It started with me waking up in the middle of the night unable to breath. If I coughed, generally this would clear things up and, although a little disturbed, I could go back to sleep. Then one night I could not clear my throat. I jumped out of bed in a blind panic and ran to the bathroom to try to forcibly get myself breathing again. This worked, but in the process I coughed up some blood. This was now enough to get me to visit the doctor.

Although it was the blood that finally got me to seek medical attention, this actually turned out to be a red herring and was just surface blood caused by the force of my coughing. After being treated for acid reflux for a period of time, it turned out that this was not the cause of the problem. After a few months, I was referred to a specialist who did all sorts of uncomfortable tests on me to eventually find out that my oesophagus pretty much does not work.

The oesophagus is the tube that connects your mouth to your stomach. It is about 10 inches long and when you swallow food, the walls of the oesophagus are supposed to squeeze together to push the food down into the stomach. Generally, on a scale of 1 to 10 this squeezing motion would have a strength of about 8 or 9. There is a condition called achalasia which in simple terms refers to a weakening of the oesophagus down to a 5 or 6 perhaps, but the tests showed that the severity of my case is that my oesophagus only operates at about a 1 or 2, if that.

I may have lived with this for years and not noticed it, but the feedback I got that night helped me to understand the condition somewhat more. When I became aware of this, it started to answer a few other questions and allowed me to make some changes. Certain stodgy foods give me more problems than others. After a few bites, I start to get feedback that I need to stop eating as everything is getting stuck in my throat. This is now instant feedback I can listen too.

Before I understood my condition, I would have still received this feedback, but because I was not clear on what it meant I was doomed to repeat it.

Another flash point for me is the time at which I eat. If I eat late at night and go to bed within less than three hours of eating, food will still be in my oesophagus and it will come back up, making me uncomfortable and possibly stop me breathing. The feedback here is a little slower. As I am eating, there is not necessarily a problem and so I continue. But an hour or so later when I go to bed and try to sleep, the feedback starts to appear. By this time it is too late and I just have to suffer through it.

This is where clarity helps. Now I know what is going on with my body, the feedback means something to me. After a few times of eating late and getting the same results, armed with my new found knowledge I can now get clear about the actions I need to take. Tracking what I eat and when I eat has been a big part of managing my condition, for which there appears to be no solution.

Feedback Your Success – Celebrate

Feedback is not only good for telling you what you are doing wrong and helping you to improve. It is also good to listen to feedback on your successes. It is common to take great actions towards your goals, only to let them pass unnoticed, but this does you a great disservice. When you do a great job you MUST celebrate. Moving straight on to the next thing on your list without appreciating your accomplishments leads to a hollow feeling that will not give you the juice and energy to take on the world. We are all much more effective when we enjoy what we do and celebrating our successes is key to this feeling.

Rituals

I have already discussed at length that in order to make any true lasting changes in your life, you need to be consistent. The best way to build consistency is to turn the activities you need to sustain into rituals. A ritual is a series of steps or habits that you put together and perform in an obsessive manner. When you take control of the rituals you perform throughout your day, you take back control of your life.

It is not always easy to know how your day is going to go. Life is a dynamic interplay with many different inputs, but what you do know is that you are going to start your day and end your day. This gives us an opportunity. Even if everything throughout the day is unpredictable, we can still create a morning ritual to run at the start of the day and an evening ritual to run at the end of the day. We can then create ad hoc rituals we can choose to run at any other time of the day whenever we have chance.

Morning Rituals

I love early mornings. I know some people do not (my wife is one of them) but I love them and the earlier I can get up, the better. The silence of having no-one else around while I get my day going is amazing. And being there as the sun rises gives me a great feeling of gratitude for the day that is about to start.

No-one who can rise before dawn, three hundred and sixty days a year fails to make his family rich.
(Chinese Proverb)

Having a morning ritual is the best way to get your day started. By creating a series of empowering activities you perform first thing in the morning before you do anything else, you go into the day feeling like you have already won and you set yourself up for success for the rest of the day. You should start off with simple rituals so you can build your consistency. The better you get at this, the more you can add and the more powerful the impact you will see on your day. Here is an example of the morning ritual I run:

- Wake at 5am
- Drink a bottle of water
- Stretch (5 minutes)
- Meditate (*) (10 minutes)

- Read or listen to inspirational material (20 minutes)
- Aerobic exercise (45 minutes)
- Weight training (60 minutes, every two days)
- Writing/content creation (90 minutes)

This ritual takes around four hours to complete if I do everything but look at how much I have accomplished before 9am when a lot of people are about to start work.

If I have an early start, or something is happening that means I do not have four hours first thing in the morning, then I can cut this back to about 60 minutes. If you cannot find 60 minutes at the start of your day, you need to rethink a few things or start getting up a little earlier! The cut down version might look like this:

- Wake at 5am
- Drink a bottle of water
- Stretch (5 minutes)
- Meditate (*) (10 minutes)
- Exercise while listening to an audio book (45 minutes)

(*) Within my rituals I highlighted the word Meditate. For me, I am not really thinking about the traditional type of meditation where you sit cross legged with your eyes closed chanting HMMMM or AHHHHH. For me, this is just about being in silence. Specifically within my morning ritual, this means climbing back into bed for ten minutes after my water and stretches so I can just lie there and let my conscious mind catch up with my subconscious mind, which has been working away while I was asleep. This can be the most powerful part of my day as so many ideas seem to come to me at this time. If it is still dark, I will use my Write by Night ™ pen with the light in the nib to scribble the ideas onto the pad that always sits on my bedside table.

Evening Rituals

Having said that your morning ritual is the very best way to start your day, it is the evening rituals that you set up and make your morning rituals possible and most powerful. I talked about starting your day the night before in the Integration Pillar, but it is worth briefly repeating it here:

Get Your Body Ready

- Watch what you eat and drink.
- Cleanse your body by not eating after 8pm.
- Set yourself up for a good night's sleep.

Get Your Mind Ready

- Plan your next day and avoid early morning thinking.
- Make exciting plans that will drag you out of bed.
- Slow everything down and use no electronics for the hour before going to bed.
- Journal and review your day for good and bad lessons.
- Write down your top ten one-year goals.
- Let your subconscious mind get to work while you sleep.

Get Your Environment Ready

- Clear your desk and declutter your office.
- Get your clothes ready for the following day.
- Put your workout clothes next to the bed.

Actions to Track

So, what can we track and what should we track?

I firmly believe that tracking is the starting point of all significant changes. Whether this be your health, your finances, your relationships or your time, if you want to improve something you should track it.

Who, reading this book, has a business? Who measures and monitors what goes on in their business? Of course, if you answered yes to the first question, you will almost certainly have answered yes to the second one. Everyone measures their profit and key performance indicators.

Now, who measures what they do in their personal life? Have you measured how many miles you ran today, how much time you spent with your kids, how many glasses of water you drank? The answer to this is probably no. No-one seems to think about measuring their life in the same way they measure their business. Most people's reaction to this is "Well it is obvious I need to do that, why would I need to record it?". Well, it is also obvious that your business needs to make a profit and that you need to be the best at customer service in your industry, but we still measure it. And why is that? Well, that too is obvious – because you need to know how you are doing so you can get even better at doing it in the future. Or you need to make sure that things are not going off track and taking you out of business.

If you were to check in with yourself on a daily basis, in the same way you check in with your business, how much better a parent could you be? How much better a friend could you be? How much better a husband or wife could you be? How much better a person could you be?

Pillar 5 – TRACKING

Whether it is simply because you want to be the best person you can be or because you want to improve your business, measuring and monitoring how you are doing is critical to moving you forward. After all, businesses are simply people, and if those people are on top of their game as individuals, you've got to believe that their businesses are going to be all the better for it.

And everything we do affects everything else – good or bad. So, by this logic, measurements and improvements in one area of your life will affect all the rest. But how will you know unless you are measuring those things too? The rider to this, of course, is that you need to remember the purpose of the measurements in the first place – and this is to improve your life. You should not be focused on the recording at the expense of getting things done and you should work on the things that matter to you.

It is very easy for someone else's urgency to get in the way of what is important to you. So, take some time to think, recognise what is important to you and start to put the building blocks in place to measure your progress.

There are many things you could measure and here are some suggestions:

1) Journal your way to a better life

Journaling is really the ultimate life tracking that anyone can do at any time. All you need is a pad of paper, a computer or maybe a leather-bound journal. If your life is worth living, it is worth recording. Words can have a magical and mystical effect and when you go deep into your own mind to examine your life, putting it into a journal can have a profound impact upon how you look at the world. With so much going on in your life, it is often difficult to make any real sense of it, but if you build the practice of writing your thoughts in a journal, you can start to develop a more cohesive view of how those thoughts fit together. Don't be like everyone else and rely on your ever-fading memory. Bring your experiences to life and immortalise them inside your journal. Supercharge the benefits you gain from recognising the patterns that shape your very existence.

Journaling and taking note of where you are today so you can see your progress in the future is a key master step to development.

As I have said elsewhere in this book, small steps in the right direction are what make all the difference in changing your life. However, it is not always easy to see those changes on a daily basis as your progress is often not perceptible from one day to the next. But when you look back six months from now, your life will be in a completely different place. However, if you had not recorded where you were, you will not be able to appreciate your progress. This also works in the other direction, of course, and if things start to slip you want to be able to spot where you are going wrong. Making journal notes of what is going on in your life is a great way to monitor this. So, take a lesson from the masters and use your experiences of today to create a better tomorrow.

2) Diets don't work!

Losing weight for the long term and keeping it off is all about lifestyle. And one of the most powerful ways of controlling your food choices and changing your lifestyle is to record everything that passes your lips. Now, recording everything you eat or drink takes some degree of diligence, least of all because you may not want to record the bad stuff, especially if you are doing it time and again. This is a constant reminder that you are not living up to your own standards. But this is exactly the point. To stop a habit in its tracks, you have to interrupt it and create an internal discomfort that will drive you to make better choices. The mere act of measuring and recording your food choices interrupts the patterns you have created within your life. A master is someone who can spot a great pattern and build from it, and at the same time recognise a bad pattern and destroy it on the spot.

If this is something that matters to you then get creative and start to measure more than just the obvious. If you want to look great and build your energy levels, don't just measure your weight. By having multiple measures, you can see your progress (or lack of progress) much more clearly. Things you could measure include:

- Weight
- Body measurements (waist, hips, arms, legs etc.)
- Body fat
- Diet
- Water intake
- Fitness levels

3) Who is in control of your emotions?

You don't have to be at the whim of the world around you. When considering this critical area of your life, come up with a list of all the positive and negative emotions you experience throughout a normal week. Keep this list at the front of your journal as reference. The next step is to measure and monitor your emotions throughout a day or preferably a week. The challenge here is to remember to do this, so why don't you set a series of alarms to go off at various times of the day and then take a minute or two to record in your journal how you are feeling and why you are feeling that way?

The objective is to spot patterns. Look at and monitor the stuff that is going on around you and examine how it is affecting the way you are feeling. There is nothing wrong with what we might term negative emotions – they are essentially calls to action – but we don't want to live there. And who doesn't want to experience more of the exciting, positive emotions we all experience once in a while? So why not learn to cultivate them on a more regular and consistent basis?

4) How much are you doing and how often are you doing it?

When thinking about what actions you should be tracking, you need to complete this statement:

I am at by best when…

For example, 'I am at my best when I run for 45 minutes first thing in the morning' or 'I am at my best when I make five sales calls every day'.

Refer to the List section of the book in the Integration Pillar and look at the section entitled Daily Habits and Rituals.

5) Time Tracking

This book is all about mastering your most valuable commodity – time. So how does your day look? What do you do during a typical day? Most people will tell you that there is no such thing as a typical day. However, if you track what you do over a seven day period, there are likely to be some patterns you can take advantage of once you understand them. The best way to do this is to track your day in 15 minute blocks, preferably over a seven day period. I like to use 15 minute blocks as this represents roughly 1% of your day.

Effectiveness

When you have worked on tracking your life and recording everything you are doing and that you need to do, you should make sure this is being done in an effective way.

There is, for sure, some work involved in getting into this level of detail, but to paraphrase Albert Einstein, if you continue to do what you have always done, you will get the same results you have always got. If you want to grow and move your life forwards, you have to be willing to make some changes. These changes are always going to start out feeling uncomfortable and they may take more time than you might like. However, you need to measure this cost in time against the benefits you get out of your life. If the benefits exceed the costs, you should just get down and do it. If the costs appear to exceed the perceived benefits then I believe you should relook at how you are approaching these changes. We can always improve, so we can make the benefits outweigh the costs.

Beware of complacency. This sneaks up on you like a thief in the night stealing away all your hard work and effort. As Jim Rohn said you need to “stand guard at the door of your mind” so you are ready to take on the world.

Build Empowering Lessons Into Your Life and Turn Cash Spent on Personal Development into Money Invested in You

Seminars, books, CDs or even conversations can provide many valuable lessons that are wasted if they are not built into your life. Yet, more than the cash involved is the time we take out of our lives to attend or study these programmes. And then we get back to our lives where within a short space of time, all of these lessons become distant memories. You must use the habit building techniques highlighted in this book to figure out a system that will ensure you never fall into this trap again. The time and money you spend will be INVESTED in you by building these lessons into your daily life and creating empowering rituals. We have all heard of the saying that Knowledge is Power. Well knowledge is not power, knowledge is only potential power. In order to make it count, you must take action NOW and build your new found knowledge into your life. We all have great intentions after we find ourselves blessed with these experiences. However, life has a bad habit of taking over and distracting us from doing the things we know we should do. Many people know what to do but it is only the few, the masters, that actually do what they know. And the time to take action is always NOW. As time passes, the enthusiasm we once felt will start to fade and the Law of Diminishing Intent will settle in. If you are waiting until the time is right, the time is never right, so just do it!

So that is what I challenge you to do now. Find one area of your life you would like to improve. Figure out exactly what your outcome would be if you had a magic wand and could not fail. Then break this down and figure out the skills you need to master in order to get to where you need to be. Start to track your activity and your progress.

Your brain is the most incredible thing in the world, but it is fallible. Your memory can play tricks on you and you don't want that to get in the way of you making progress and becoming the person you want to be, or indeed the person you want your friends and family to see you as.

There is an enormous amount going on in all our lives. Time flies by so quickly that it very easy to forget what you have done from one day to the next. At the end of the week who knows how many times you really exercised, or how many glasses of water you drank, or how long you spent truly connecting to your partner or children. The only way you can reliably know these things is if you record them. You need to make sure that what you are measuring matters, but let's face it, everything matters; some things just matter more than others.

Pillar 5 – TRACKING

Daily Life Tracker ®

Throughout the book I have mentioned Daily Life Tracker ® (DLT). This is my own unique personal development and life management software which has been designed to be the only tool or system you need to manage and take control of your whole life. It was designed around two key principles: 'what gets measured gets done' and 'ordinary activities consistently performed produce extraordinary results'.

Whilst DLT is a tool, the principles of DLT are a lifestyle. It's a habit formation tool that helps you create good habits and get rid of bad habits.

It is also a life tracking tool that enables you to track and manage all your daily activities, which is all about habit formation. It allows you to track and manage your diet, your weight, your body measurements, your fitness levels and anything else going on in your whole life. You can also track and manage your life goals and all the actions you have to do throughout your day, and even throughout your life. But it isn't just a life tracker. It can also be used to track and manage your business's key performance indicators and specific events such as medical issues, running a marathon or preparing for exams. In fact, it tracks anything where you have repeated actions over multiple disciplines.

It is also a life balancing tool. But not just work-life balance, whole-life balance:

i. Health

ii. Finance

iii. Relationships

iv. Emotions

v. Personal development

vi. Life management

You see, it's all about pattern recognition and with everything you are able to record inside Daily Life Tracker ®, you will start to spot patterns.

Essentially, it is a tool that will help you to manage your life and lifestyle. But first you must get everything out of your head and into Daily Life Tracker ®. This frees your brain to do what it is supposed to do, which is to be creative. Your brain wasn't designed to store all the things you have to do today. Life is far too complex. But, once you get everything out of your head and into Daily Life Tracker ®, this can start to get a little scary because now you have got to start to think for yourself. You see, for most people, their inbox and the world around them is in control of their lives and what they do next. But once you get everything out of your head and into Daily Life Tracker® (and I mean everything) then you get to decide what to do next because basically you have everything under control. This is where it gets quite scary – but ultimately and at the same time, it is absolutely liberating. If you get everything out of your head and into the Daily Life Tracker® system, your creativity will explode.

Daily Life Tracker ® is where my business began. It was created for me because I was becoming a seminar junkie, looking for big bangs and magic bullets that were going to change my life in an instant. And then, after speaking with my coach, I had this blinding flash of the obvious that it was never the big shifts I was looking for. My true growth was going to come in the small daily activities I performed each day. So I developed a system that allowed me to tick off actions I did every day to help me build better and better habits. Then I turned it into a spreadsheet, then a database and then, over several years, into the incredible online application it is today.

My success and everything I have today is in no small part down to the habits I have built using Daily Life Tracker ®. I know the results you can get if you take the principles outlined in this book and apply them to your life through the medium of Daily Life Tracker ® and it is nothing short of game changing!

We all need to be held accountable for our actions otherwise it is easy to become complacent and not push ourselves as hard as we should. Daily Life Tracker ® acts as your personal accountability partner, which sits there on your laptop or mobile device 24 hours a day, 7 days a week, 365 days a year. It is great to have another human being holding us to account but even the best coach or friend cannot be there every minute of the day. They cannot follow through with you on every little aspect you want to improve. For that Daily Life Tracker ® is just the ticket.

If you have only a couple of things you need to master, you can probably manage without a system. However, if you truly want to take control of all the different elements of your life and address them in the consistent manner that is needed for true mastery, you need something to help you. Daily Life Tracker ® will help you build that consistency. There are no prizes for dabblers and Daily Life Tracker ® will make sure you follow through if you commit to using it.

Daily Life Tracker ® Features

- Habit Formation/Goal Setting Functionality
- To-Do List

- Diet Tracker
- Body Tracker
- Fitness Tracker
- Sleep Tracker
- Journal

Go to www.dailylifetracker.com and sign up for a copy today.

Pillar 5 – TRACKING

The 5 Pillars in Action

- Create your morning rituals.
- Create your evening rituals.
- Start to keep a journal every day.
- Get hold of a copy of Daily Life Tracker ® and take control of your life NOW.

Conclusion

Conclusion

You must always push yourself to be the very best you can be. I am a firm believer that competition is not about the other guy. Competition is an internal thing. If you are capable of being number one then anything less than that is simply not good enough. However, if you are surrounded by superstars and you do your absolute best and come in at number four, then that is perfect.

The best competition I have is against myself, to become better. *(John Wooden)*

However, at the same time I am all about making it as easy as possible. Not because I am lazy and don't want to do the work, but because I know that this is the best way to keep you motivated and taking action. If you go out for a run and go so hard at it that you cannot breathe and you are sweating blood then there is every chance that you are not going to go back out there. Push yourself, yes, but make sure you can push yourself consistently.

I was taught this by one of my mentors, Stu Mittleman. If you have followed Tony Robbins at all, you have probably heard of Stu. He coached Tony for a while and still speaks at some of his events. Now, Stu is awesome and if you look into the sorts of things he did when he was competing, you would realise that he is probably one of the craziest people on the planet! Stu is the former world champion and world record holder at what can only be described as the crazy distance of 1,000 miles. He was only the sixth American to be inducted into the American Ultrarunning Hall of Fame. Stu is clearly someone who pushes himself way beyond the limits of what anyone would expect of him.

But even with that background, Stu will tell you that you need to operate at a level that works for you. If you push too hard, it will work for the moment but over time it will catch up with you. Easy simple steps are what it takes. One of the greatest lessons I learned from Stu was set in the context of me getting ready to run a marathon. Stu would always say that your goal is Consistency, Duration, Intensity – in that order.

This works the same in life as it does in running. You will get your best and longest lasting results by consistently performing the simple everyday tasks.

Remember, any time you save by being more productive gets converted into anything you choose to focus on, so choose wisely.

It may seem that there is a lot to think about within these pages but remember there are only five Pillars and six Life Categories you need to focus on. Your best friend is your consistency. Day by day, step by step, simple actions that will change your life. This will take you further forward than anything else you have learned.

I have said it before and I will say it again, "Ordinary activities consistently performed produce extraordinary results!"

Now let's get out there and get started.

If you empty your purse into your head, no-one can take it away from you. An investment in knowledge always pays best interest.
(Benjamin Franklin)

Conclusion

Recommendations

Think and Grow Rich (Napoleon Hill)

The 7 Habits of Highly Effective People (Stephen Covey)

How to Win Friends and Influence People (Dale Carnegie)

The Richest Man in Babylon (George S Clason)

Leading an Inspired Life (Jim Rohn)

The Compound Effect (Darren Hardy)

Life Leverage (Rob Moore)

Getting Things Done (David Allen)

The Procrastination Equation (Dr Piers Steel)

The Power of Habit (Charles Duhigg)

Personal Power (Tony Robbins)

Awaken the Giant Within (Tony Robbins)

[Anything you can find by Tony Robbins]

Eat That Frog (Brian Tracy)

Laws of Success (Les Brown)

Live Your Dreams (Les Brown)

Ready Fire Aim (Michael Masterson)

Slow Burn (Stu Mittleman)

Additional Support

For more information and to get access to Daily Life Tracker ®, our proprietary software which will help you to embed all these principles into your life faster than you ever believed possible, visit us at:

www.productivitypowerhouse.com

www.dailylifetracker.com

or contact me personally at:

carl@productivitypowerhouse.com